AMERICA'S —
TEST KITCHEN

praise for america's test kitchen titles

"This book upgrades slow cooking for discriminating, 21st-century palates—that is indeed revolutionary."
THE DALLAS MORNING NEWS ON *SLOW COOKER REVOLUTION*

"This book begins with a detailed buying guide, a critical summary of available sizes and attachments, and a list of clever food processor techniques. Easy and versatile dishes follow . . . Both new and veteran food processor owners will love this practical guide."
LIBRARY JOURNAL ON *FOOD PROCESSOR PERFECTION*

"Another winning cookbook from ATK. . . . The folks at America's Test Kitchen apply their rigorous experiments to determine the facts about these pans."
BOOKLIST ON *COOK IT IN CAST IRON*

"This impressive installment from America's Test Kitchen equips readers with dozens of repertoire-worthy recipes. . . . This is a must-have for beginner cooks and more experienced ones who wish to sharpen their skills."
PUBLISHERS WEEKLY (STARRED REVIEW) ON
THE NEW ESSENTIALS COOKBOOK

"This encyclopedia of meat cookery would feel completely overwhelming if it weren't so meticulously organized and artfully designed. This is Cook's Illustrated at its finest."
THE KITCHN ON *THE COOK'S ILLUSTRATED MEAT BOOK*

Selected as the Cookbook Award Winner of 2017 in the Baking Category
INTERNATIONAL ASSOCIATION OF CULINARY PROFESSIONALS (IACP) ON *BREAD ILLUSTRATED*

"With 1,000 photos and the expertise of the America's Test Kitchen editors, this title might be the definitive book on bread baking."
PUBLISHERS WEEKLY ON *BREAD ILLUSTRATED*

Selected as one of the 10 Best New Cookbooks of 2017
THE LA TIMES ON *THE PERFECT COOKIE*

"The book offers an impressive education for curious cake makers, new and experienced alike. A summation of 25 years of cake making at ATK, there are cakes for every taste."
THE WALL STREET JOURNAL ON *THE PERFECT CAKE*

Selected as one of Amazon's Best Books of 2015 in the Cookbooks and Food Writing Category
AMAZON ON *THE COMPLETE VEGETARIAN COOKBOOK*

"The 21st-century *Fannie Farmer Cookbook* or *The Joy of Cooking*. If you had to have one cookbook and that's all you could have, this one would do it."
CBS SAN FRANCISCO ON *THE NEW FAMILY COOKBOOK*

"The go-to gift book for newlyweds, small families, or empty nesters."
ORLANDO SENTINEL ON *THE COMPLETE COOKING FOR TWO COOKBOOK*

"The sum total of exhaustive experimentation . . . anyone interested in gluten-free cookery simply shouldn't be without it."
NIGELLA LAWSON ON *THE HOW CAN IT BE GLUTEN-FREE COOKBOOK*

"A one-volume kitchen seminar, addressing in one smart chapter after another the sometimes surprising whys behind a cook's best practices. . . . You get the myth, the theory, the science, and the proof, all rigorously interrogated as only America's Test Kitchen can do."
NPR ON *THE SCIENCE OF GOOD COOKING*

"Some 2,500 photos walk readers through 600 painstakingly tested recipes, leaving little room for error."
ASSOCIATED PRESS ON *THE AMERICA'S TEST KITCHEN COOKING SCHOOL COOKBOOK*

"This book is a comprehensive, no-nonsense guide . . . a well-thought-out, clearly explained primer for every aspect of home baking."
THE WALL STREET JOURNAL ON *THE COOK'S ILLUSTRATED BAKING BOOK*

AIR FRYER
PERFECTION

From Crispy Fries and Juicy Steaks to Perfect Vegetables
WHAT TO COOK AND HOW TO GET THE BEST RESULTS

America's Test Kitchen

Library of Congress Cataloging-in-Publication Data
Names: America's Test Kitchen (Firm), author.
Title: Air fryer perfection : from crispy fries and juicy steaks to perfect
    vegetables : what to cook & how to get the best results / America's
    Test Kitchen.
Description: Boston, MA : America's Test Kitchen, [2019] | Includes
    bibliographical references and index.
Identifiers: LCCN 2018040107 | ISBN 9781945256752
Subjects: LCSH: Hot air frying. | LCGFT: Cookbooks.
Classification: LCC TX689 .A485 2019 | DDC 641.7/7--dc23
LC record available at https://lccn.loc.gov/2018040107

America's Test Kitchen
21 Drydock Avenue, Boston, MA 02210

Manufactured in the United States of America

10 9 8 7 6 5 4 3 2 1

Distributed by Penguin Random House Publisher Services
Tel: 800.733.3000

Pictured on front cover: French Fries (page 161), Lamb Kofte Wraps (page 108), Roasted Salmon Fillets with Mango-Mint Salsa (page 125), Crispy Breaded Boneless Pork Chops (page 87), Flank Steak with Roasted Potatoes and Chimichurri (page 66), Chicken Nuggets (page 18)

Pictured on back cover (clockwise from top left):
Vietnamese-Style Rice Noodle Salad with Pork (page 99), Cheesy Potatoes (page 158), South Carolina–Style Shrimp Bake (page 139), Buffalo Chicken Drumsticks (page 54), Southwestern Bean and Corn Hand Pies (page 84).

Editorial Director, Books ELIZABETH CARDUFF

Executive Editor ADAM KOWIT

Executive Food Editor DAN ZUCCARELLO

Deputy Food Editor STEPHANIE PIXLEY

Senior Editor NICOLE KONSTANTINAKOS

Associate Editors AFTON CYRUS, LAWMAN JOHNSON, AND RUSSELL SELANDER

Test Cooks CAMILA CHAPARRO AND KATHERINE PERRY

Assistant Editor KELLY GAUTHIER

Art Director LINDSEY CHANDLER

Deputy Art Directors COURTNEY LENTZ AND JANET TAYLOR

Associate Art Director KATIE BARRANGER

Photography Director JULIE BOZZO COTE

Photography Producer MEREDITH MULCAHY

Senior Staff Photographer DANIEL J. VAN ACKERE

Staff Photographers STEVE KLISE AND KEVIN WHITE

Additional Photography KELLER + KELLER AND CARL TREMBLAY

Food Styling TARA BUSA, CATRINE KELTY, CHANTAL LAMBETH, KENDRA MCKNIGHT, MARIE PIRAINO, ELLE SIMONE SCOTT, KENDRA SMITH, AND SALLY STAUB

Photoshoot Kitchen Team

    Photo Team and Special Events Manager TIMOTHY MCQUINN

    Lead Test Cook DANIEL CELLUCCI

    Test Cook JESSICA RUDOLPH

    Assistant Test Cooks SARAH EWALD, ERIC HAESSLER, AND DEVON SHATKIN

Illustration JAY LAYMAN

Production Manager CHRISTINE SPANGER

Imaging Manager LAUREN ROBBINS

Production and Imaging Specialists DENNIS NOBLE, JESSICA VOAS, AND AMANDA YONG

Copy Editor JEFFREY SCHIER

Proofreader JANE TUNKS DEMEL

Indexer ELIZABETH PARSON

Chief Creative Officer JACK BISHOP

Executive Editorial Directors JULIA COLLIN DAVISON AND BRIDGET LANCASTER

CONTENTS

WELCOME TO AMERICA'S TEST KITCHEN

This book has been tested, written, and edited by the folks at America's Test Kitchen. Located in Boston's Seaport District in the historic Innovation and Design Building, it features 15,000 square feet of kitchen space including multiple photography and video studios. It is the home of *Cook's Illustrated* magazine and *Cook's Country* magazine and is the workday destination for more than 60 test cooks, editors, and cookware specialists. Our mission is to test recipes over and over again until we understand how and why they work and until we arrive at the best version.

We start the process of testing a recipe with a complete lack of preconceptions, which means that we accept no claim, no technique, and no recipe at face value. We simply assemble as many variations as possible, test a half-dozen of the most promising, and taste the results blind. We then construct our own recipe and continue to test it, varying ingredients, techniques, and cooking times until we reach a consensus. As we like to say in the test kitchen, "We make the mistakes so you don't have to." The result, we hope, is the best version of a particular recipe, but we realize that only you can be the final judge of our success (or failure). We use the same rigorous approach when we test equipment and taste ingredients.

All of this would not be possible without a belief that good cooking, much like good music, is based on a foundation of objective technique. Some people like spicy foods and others don't, but there is a right way to sauté, there is a best way to cook a pot roast, and there are measurable scientific principles involved in producing perfectly beaten, stable egg whites. Our ultimate goal is to investigate the fundamental principles of cooking to give you the techniques, tools, and ingredients you need to become a better cook. It is as simple as that.

To see what goes on behind the scenes at America's Test Kitchen, check out our social media channels for kitchen snapshots, exclusive content, video tips, and much more. You can watch us work (in our actual test kitchen) by tuning in to *America's Test Kitchen* or *Cook's Country from America's Test Kitchen* on public television or on our websites. Listen in to test kitchen experts on public radio (SplendidTable.org) to hear insights that illuminate the truth about real home cooking. Want to hone your cooking skills or finally learn how to bake—with an America's Test Kitchen test cook? Enroll in one of our online cooking classes. However you choose to visit us, we welcome you into our kitchen, where you can stand by our side as we test our way to the best recipes in America.

facebook.com/AmericasTestKitchen

twitter.com/TestKitchen

youtube.com/AmericasTestKitchen

instagram.com/TestKitchen

pinterest.com/TestKitchen

google.com/+AmericasTestKitchen

AmericasTestKitchen.com

CooksIllustrated.com

CooksCountry.com

OnlineCookingSchool.com

AIR FRYER 101

INTRODUCTION

In the past few years air fryers have taken over store shelves and TV commercials, with a seemingly endless stream of new models. The rise of air fryers is easy to understand given their promise of healthier fried foods, but we weren't about to make room in our kitchen for an appliance that could produce only French fries, no matter how good. Could this gizmo be taken seriously? To start, we needed to understand exactly what an air fryer was and how we could use this unique cooking method to our advantage.

Despite the clever name, an air fryer is not a fryer at all. It's a mini convection oven that cooks food by circulating hot air around it with a fan. The genius of the method is that food cooked by convection can approach the crispiness of fried food while using far less oil (at least when cooked properly; you can also simply dry food out, as we learned). But the intense hot air is also ideal for roasting and even allows us to prepare dishes we might otherwise cook on the grill. Viewed in this light, the air fryer started to sound more appealing. If it could make dinner—not just snacks—with less mess and fuss (and in less time) than if we used our oven, we reasoned, it might well be worth the space on our counter. So, while skeptical, we assembled a lineup of air fryers and started testing.

The more we tasted, the more we found ourselves liking the air fryer. Rosy steaks, juicy chicken, vibrant asparagus, and pillowy potato wedges with crisp edges all emerged from the basket and were devoured. Colleagues in the test kitchen would stop by and ask, "Did you make that in the air fryer?" before stealing a bite. The best part was the ease: There was no splattering, and the device could mostly be left alone. Our favorite model even turned itself off after the timer dinged. Finicky dishes like bone-in chicken breasts became close to effortless thanks to the controlled temperature and timer. And we appreciated that when we were cooking for two people (as many of us are on some nights) the air fryer provided just the amount we needed without the leftovers or the fuss of making a larger dish. Even simple fare like baked potatoes felt easier in the air fryer. After all, the spuds can hog oven space for upward of an hour. Using the air fryer left our oven free for whatever main dish we might want to make.

But more often we were lured by the promise of creating a full meal using only the air fryer. In some cases, we used the downtime while our main dish was cooking in the air fryer to prepare a simple side, such as with our Lemon-Oregano Roasted Pork Chops with Tomato-Feta Salad (page 91) or Beef Satay with Red Curry Noodles (page 76). We also found ways to cook a complete meal inside the air fryer, perching pork tenderloins over cubed butternut squash, or laying moist cod fillets over roasted potatoes, orchestrating the timing so everything finished together.

Did you know that you can cook a version of spaghetti and meatballs in the air fryer? See page 79. Cheesy potato gratin? See page 158. We air-fried cheeseburgers (far less messy than using a skillet). We got fancy and roasted boneless beef short ribs; in the air fryer's powerful heat, they emerged rich and luscious—a restaurant-quality meal involving barely any work. On the flip side, knowing how well frozen food crisps up in the air fryer, we developed homemade takes on freezer-aisle favorites that we could make ahead and air-fry whenever the craving struck.

Despite its convenience, the air fryer isn't magic. Getting great results involved more than simply closing the basket and turning it on. (We tried that many times, and more often than not were met with bland, limp, and poorly or unevenly browned food.) Like all equipment, it benefits from the right techniques. Through testing, we learned the secrets to producing air-fried chicken with a golden crust, Brussels sprouts that tasted like they came out of a deep fryer, and French fries that raised the bar on what can be achieved without a pot of bubbling oil: Ours come out crisp, fluffy, and irresistible.

We've incorporated all of the tips, discoveries, and secrets we learned in the test kitchen to create recipes that work in every air fryer, every time. In the following pages you'll learn how to cook crispy, evenly browned, and well-roasted food whether you've been air-frying for a while or are a complete novice. With this guide for success, you'll see why we now count the air fryer among our most well-loved appliances.

TEN REASONS WE LIKE THE AIR FRYER

1 It produces real food Since it's essentially a small convection oven, the air fryer can cook many of the foods you might roast or bake with less fuss. The basket's wire base helps food to cook evenly since air circulates on all sides.

2 Less-fat frying Yes, the air fryer's intended purpose holds true: Instead of quarts of oil, we can use just a small amount and achieve beautifully crisp results for French fries, chicken, fish, and more.

3 Set and (almost) forget Unlike stovetop cooking, air frying requires virtually no monitoring, thanks to its well-regulated temperature and automatic shutoff. Other than the occasional flip or toss, it does all the work, allowing you to focus on the rest of the meal.

4 Minimal mess The food basket is enclosed in the air fryer, and this translates to a clean kitchen—no splattering oil or multiple dirty pots and pans. Plus, the baskets are simple to clean—most are nonstick and dishwasher-safe.

5 No stove—or oven—needed On busy nights when we must convince ourselves to cook (even test cooks feel this way at times), not having to turn on the stove can be a blessing. And on hot nights, the air fryer keeps our kitchen from becoming a steam room.

6 It's fast The air fryer lets us skip past the common first step in cooking—heating fat in a pan or heating the oven or grill. This not only was convenient but also shaved valuable time off of our recipes.

7 Easy meals for kids The ability to crisp up a batch of chicken nuggets, bake a couple of hand pies, or roast carrots without embarking on a cooking project makes this a lifesaver for busy parents.

8 Ideal for two people When it's just the two of you eating (or you're cooking solo) and you don't want to make more than you need, the air fryer helps to prevent waste. Our recipes were made with standard air-fryer basket sizes in mind, and many yield two servings.

9 Your automated sous chef Cooking multiple dishes in the oven can be a juggling act. Hand a side dish over to the air fryer and free up valuable space.

10 Even results All of the previous benefits would amount to null if the air fryer's cooking results were spotty, but we continued to be surprised at how good the food tasted. The most common remark we heard at recipe tastings was, "I can't believe this came from an air fryer!"

ANATOMY OF A GREAT AIR FRYER

Peer inside an air fryer and you may not immediately be able to tell what makes it work. Here we illuminate the key elements found in many air fryers and point out the attributes that we liked in our winning model.

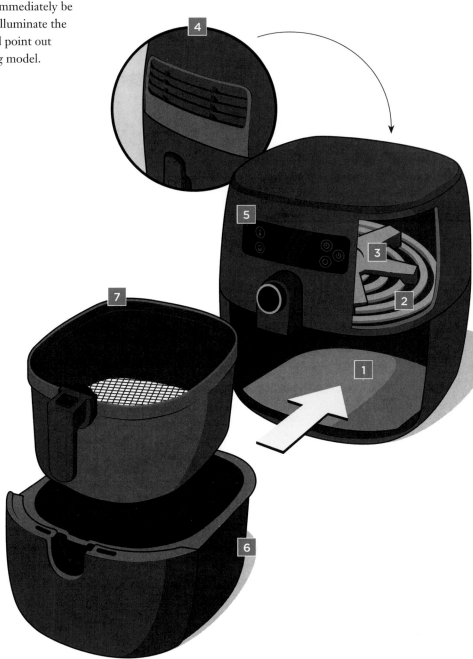

WHAT IF MY AIR FRYER LOOKS DIFFERENT?

While air fryers come in many shapes and sizes, and can even vary in how the food is placed inside, they all operate in a similar way. If your air fryer model doesn't have all the features we mention here, don't fret: We've tested our recipes in a variety of models to ensure that they will work in every air fryer.

Not all air-fryer drawers are removable, and some models load from the top rather than the front and do not have a drawer at all. Be sure to read your air fryer's instruction manual to check whether the drawer is removable. Some air fryers have tiered racks or shelves rather than a basket. You can make all of our recipes in this type of air fryer by using the bottom rack or shelf for cooking.

Some brands of air fryers come in extra-large (XL) sizes; these have a bigger drawer capacity. All our recipes will work in XL air fryers, but we crafted them with standard-size air fryers in mind, so an XL model is not necessary.

CHOOSING THE RIGHT TEMPERATURE AND TIME FOR YOUR AIR FRYER

Because settings vary slightly among air fryers, we tested our recipes in multiple models and asked our readers to test recipes too. Here are some guidelines to follow.

Temperature: Different air fryers use different temperature increments, increasing by 10, 25, or even 30 degrees. If your air fryer cannot be set to the specified temperature, select the closest available temperature setting.

Time: Always check food for doneness at the low end of the time range and add time as necessary. The cook time range given in a recipe takes into account the slight differences between models.

1 Chamber
The rounded chamber promotes air circulation. Our winning air fryer had adequate space both above and below the basket, which helped the hot air to flow around all sides of the food.

2 Heating element
An electric coil located above the basket heats the air fryer's small space much faster than an oven can.

3 Fan
Air fryers, like convection ovens, use fans to circulate heat around food for faster and more even cooking.

4 Exhaust
An exhaust at the back of the air fryer releases some of the hot air to prevent the pressure and heat inside the chamber from getting too high.

5 Controls
Dial or touchscreen controls allow you to select temperatures and set cook times. We prefer digital dials and flat displays that can't be bumped or that have to be confirmed before the cooking temperature is changed.

6 Drawer
Also called a pan, the drawer found in most air fryers is the container for the basket. Excess oil and drippings will collect at the bottom. We liked models with removable drawers for easy cleanup.

7 Basket
Most air fryers contain a nonstick basket that suspends food in the chamber so air can flow around it. We liked the roomy, square shape of our winning air fryer's basket, which made it easy to space out food.

AIR FRYER Q&A

Do I need to preheat the air fryer?

Our recipes don't require preheating. An air fryer heats much faster than an oven. We found that the total time it took to cook food started in a cold air fryer was the same as when we waited a few minutes for the air fryer to heat and then added our food; plus, skipping the preheating was convenient.

How much can an air fryer hold?

Most standard air fryers can fit enough food for 2 to 4 servings, depending on the food. We kept the air fryer's size in mind as we developed our recipes and made sure not to overcrowd the basket. If you choose to make multiple batches of a recipe, start checking the second batch for doneness a few minutes early, as the air fryer will already be hot and may cook the second batch more quickly.

Do I need the extras and attachments?

Some air fryers come with attachments such as racks and pans. While these can be useful for specific purposes, our recipes were crafted to use only the basic air-fryer basket.

How do I prevent food from sticking?

For foods that are prone to sticking, such as breaded chicken or delicate fish, we recommend spraying the basket lightly with vegetable oil spray. Using a foil sling can also make cleanup and the removal of certain foods easier, especially fish (for information on making a foil sling, see page 11).

CLEANING YOUR AIR FRYER

Most removable parts of the air fryer, such as the drawer and basket of many models, are dishwasher-safe, but you should consult your air-fryer manual before putting parts in the dishwasher. The main body of your air fryer also needs to be cleaned occasionally, as grease and food splatters can build up around the heating element and cause smoking. Turning the air fryer upside down can make it easier to access the heating element of some models. Make sure your air fryer is completely cool before you clean the inside, and use a mild detergent. After you clean the air fryer, briefly run it to dry out the inside.

TESTING AIR FRYERS

Air fryers offer a bold promise: perfectly fried food using very little oil (often less than a tablespoon). While we've never been shy about frying (which usually requires cups or even quarts of oil), a gadget that promises to do the job faster, with less oil, and with less mess sure seemed appealing. But did the air fryer's claim have merit or was it just marketing? To find out, we tested a variety of air fryers, priced from $60.20 to $249.95, using each to cook a variety of foods.

Taking the Air Fryer's Temperature

Before we could even start comparing results from various air fryer models, we had to overcome a learning curve. Making food according to manufacturers' recommendations mostly resulted in undercooked food such as soggy French fries. But adapted versions of our own oven recipes often came out overcooked and dry. For many dishes, the optimal cooking times and temperatures fell somewhere between those of our oven recipes and manufacturers' instructions. As we homed in on these, we started turning out crispy fries, juicy chicken parts, and tender chicken cutlets.

Most air fryers we tried maxed out at about 400 degrees, a bit below what we recommend in our recipes for oven-fried foods. This wasn't a problem, though, because air fryers convey heat more efficiently than traditional ovens do. Since a fan is constantly circulating the air, the food usually cooks faster. Once we made adjustments—typically using a lower temperature and less time—we were able to get crispy fries and tender chicken a few minutes faster than in the oven. We were also pleasantly surprised to find that the small, fast-heating air fryers don't need to be preheated, which shaved additional minutes off our total cooking time.

Ultimately, the food held its own against oven-fried versions—and was often better as well as more convenient to prepare. Fries were crispy on the outside and fluffy on the inside, and chicken Parmesan had a crunchy crust and bubbly, browned cheese. With the exception of one air fryer that gave off a rancid oil smell that permeated the food (the company says this is manufacturing grease that should burn off in one to two uses, but we found that it was still lingering after nine tests and multiple washings), all the air fryers produced really good, crispy food.

A Good Air Fryer Is Both Safe and Easy to Use

Although all the air fryers cooked food well, usability was a different story. Even though air fryers are constantly circulating air, the cooking isn't completely hands-off; you still need to turn or toss food during cooking to promote even browning, at least in most cases. Still, a few air fryers required more attention than others.

Some air fryers had analog dials for setting cooking temperatures; these were very easy and intuitive to use, but we often knocked them out of place and inadvertently changed the heat setting whenever we opened or moved the unit. Testers preferred digital dials and displays that were flat and couldn't be bumped or that had to be confirmed before the cooking temperature was changed.

Other models had "innovations" that ranged from benign—presets for foods such as French fries and fish, which we found mostly useless—to downright baffling, such as an air fryer with a mixing paddle that sliced right through French fries, a machine with 11 different attachments but no handle to lift out the basket, and one model with its own temperature system of "levels 1–4" but without any mention of degrees.

Inserts that were hard to clean were also a no-go: One air fryer's thin, mesh-like basket was made from metal that stained, ripped our sponge, and warped when we tried to clean it. We preferred sturdy nonstick surfaces that cleaned up effortlessly.

Air fryers are also big—in most cases larger than a full-size food processor. In rating models, we focused on standard-size fryers rather than on the big XL models. Even so, some models were gigantic (up to a foot and a half wide), hogging a whole counter's worth of space, with flip-up lids that banged into our cabinets when we tried to open them. Because they had such a wide footprint, we expected an extra-large capacity, but most of these larger units could hold only a bit more than smaller air fryers (about three chicken cutlets rather than two). We preferred slimmer, shorter machines that gave us more room on our counters.

We also preferred drawer-style models, which had a front-facing basket that pulled out like a drawer, to flip-top models. Drawer-style air fryers not only took up less space but also were much safer: Most flip-top products had heating elements in their lids that were completely exposed when the unit was open—and their heavy lids threatened to drop those heating elements right onto our hands. We liked how drawer-style air fryers kept their heating elements hidden up and away in the machine, a big boon to safety.

The Best Air Fryer to Buy

Our favorite air fryer was the most expensive one in our lineup, the Philips TurboStar Airfryer, Avance Digital ($249.95). We loved its slimmer footprint, which maxed out at about 14 inches. Its digital controls were easy to use, and cooking was all-around effortless. However, if you have 2 more inches of under-cabinet clearance and are willing to sacrifice the intuitive controls, we can recommend the GoWISE USA 3.7-Quart 7-in-1 Air Fryer ($75.15). This drawer-style model also produced great food at a more affordable price; it's our Best Buy.

WINNING TRAITS IN AN AIR FRYER

- Makes evenly cooked, crispy food in less time than in a conventional oven

- Smaller footprint and shorter frame that don't hog counters or obstruct cabinets

- Pullout cooking drawer and concealed heating element to minimize the risk of burning yourself

- Surface and handle that stay cool to the touch, even when cooking at higher temperatures

- Digital controls for precise temperature and timer control

- Automatically stops cooking when timer ends

- Nonstick surface for easy cleaning

recommended	performance	comments

Philips
TurboStar Airfryer,
Avance Digital

MODEL HD9641/96
PRICE $249.95
CONTROLS Digital
STYLE Drawer
HEIGHT 11 in
MAXIMUM WIDTH 14.5 in
MAXIMUM TEMPERATURE 400°
DISHWASHER-SAFE Yes

COOKING ★★★
EASE OF USE ★★★
CLEANUP ★★★
SIZE ★★★
SAFETY ★★★

Testers loved this machine, which had a slimmer, compact footprint and a shorter stature and thus took up less room on our counters. Its basket was roomy and had a completely nonstick coating. We liked that the bottom of the basket could be removed for even deeper cleaning. Its digital controls and dial-operated menu made setting the temperature and time easy and intuitive. The machine stopped cooking as soon as the set time was up, and its drawer-like design allowed us to remove food without exposing our hands to the heating element.

GoWISE USA
3.7-Quart 7-in-1 Air Fryer
`BEST BUY`

MODEL GW22621
PRICE $75.15
CONTROLS Digital
STYLE Drawer
HEIGHT 13 in
MAXIMUM WIDTH 13 in
MAXIMUM TEMPERATURE 400°
DISHWASHER-SAFE Yes

COOKING ★★★
EASE OF USE ★★½
CLEANUP ★★★
SIZE ★★★
SAFETY ★★★

While this air fryer's digital controls weren't quite as intuitive as those of our favorite model, it was still easy to set the time and temperature once we got the hang of the multiple buttons. It cooked quickly and produced crisp foods, and its display was bright, large, and easy to read. Though it's a little bigger than our favorite model, it was still short enough to fit under our cabinets, and its drawer-style design and automatic shutoff were a boon to safety. Like other models, it had a non-stick interior, which was easy to clean.

Philips
TurboStar Airfryer, Viva Analog

MODEL HD9621/96
PRICE $199.95
CONTROLS Analog
STYLE Drawer
HEIGHT 11 in
MAXIMUM WIDTH 14.5 in
MAXIMUM TEMPERATURE 400°
DISHWASHER-SAFE Yes

COOKING ★★★
EASE OF USE ★★
CLEANUP ★★★
SIZE ★★★
SAFETY ★★★

This analog air fryer had all the charm of our favorite digital model by Philips, including a smaller stature and footprint, a roomy cooking basket, and nonstick materials that were a breeze to clean. It cooked evenly and speedily, performing alongside our top pick in every cooking test. We had only a few quibbles: Its analog timer dial wasn't as precise as digital controls, and its temperature dial occasionally got knocked out of place, changing the temperature, when we moved the unit or checked on food.

Rosewill
RHAF-15004 1400W Oil-Less
Low Fat Air Fryer - 3.3-Quart
(3.2L), Black

MODEL RHAF-15004
PRICE $60.20
CONTROLS Analog
STYLE Drawer
HEIGHT 12 in
MAXIMUM WIDTH 14.8 in
MAXIMUM TEMPERATURE 400°
DISHWASHER-SAFE Yes

COOKING ★★★
EASE OF USE ★★
CLEANUP ★★★
SIZE ★★½
SAFETY ★★★

Another shorter, drawer-style air fryer that could fit easily under cabinets, this analog model had simple controls that were intuitive to set. While it cooked food well and cleaned up easily, testers struggled a bit when sliding the basket into the machine, and it required some jiggering to lock in. As with other analog models, its temperature dial was easy to knock slightly away from the target temperature.

recommended with reservations	performance	comments

Kalorik
Airfryer with Dual Layer Rack

MODEL FT 42139 BK
PRICE $89.99
CONTROLS Analog
STYLE Drawer
HEIGHT 13 in
MAXIMUM WIDTH 13.4 in
MAXIMUM TEMPERATURE 400°
DISHWASHER-SAFE Yes

COOKING ★★★
EASE OF USE ★
CLEANUP ★★★
SIZE ★★½
SAFETY ★★★

This basic analog model was compact and easy to use—at least until the timer stopped working. Though the air fryer came with a 1-year warranty, the company was unresponsive to calls and messages left with the warranty line. A subsequent model we tried didn't have this problem, however, and made food that was crispy. It also came with a rack for cooking two layers of food, which is good for foods such as French fries that need a bit more room to crisp up.

not recommended	performance	comments

Black+Decker
2 Liter Purifry Air Fryer

MODEL HF100WD
PRICE $74.99
CONTROLS Analog
STYLE Drawer
HEIGHT 13.2 in
MAXIMUM WIDTH 14 in
MAXIMUM TEMPERATURE 400°
DISHWASHER-SAFE Yes

COOKING ★
EASE OF USE ★★½
CLEANUP ★★★
SIZE ★★½
SAFETY ★★★

This analog model was effortless to get up and running: no frills, no presets, just simple time and temperature dials. While it made crispy fries and chicken, we were dismayed by the burnt-plastic smell it gave off when cooking, which permeated the food and left it inedible. Though the manual said that this smell is from manufacturing grease and should go away within one to two uses, we noticed it nine tests later, after multiple long cooking projects and washings. Its analog timer dial was also a bit difficult to set precisely.

De'Longhi
Multifry

MODEL FH1163
PRICE $175.22
CONTROLS Analog
STYLE Flip-top
HEIGHT 10 in
MAXIMUM WIDTH 14.5 in
MAXIMUM TEMPERATURE
"Level 4"
DISHWASHER-SAFE Yes

COOKING ★★
EASE OF USE ★
CLEANUP ★★★
SIZE ★★★
SAFETY ★½

Testers appreciated this flip-top air fryer's shorter profile, which allowed it to fit under cabinets even when opened, and its see-through top. But this machine was rife with issues, including confusing buttons and a "levels 1–4" temperature system that offered no guidance as to corresponding actual temperatures. A paddle attachment meant to stir the food as it cooked ended up mangling French fries. The timer was nearly impossible to see and hear, and the machine didn't stop cooking when the timer expired.

Gourmia
FreeFry 360 TurboXP Cookcenter

MODEL GTA2500
PRICE $168.00
CONTROLS Digital
STYLE Flip-top
HEIGHT 13 in
MAXIMUM WIDTH 17 in
MAXIMUM TEMPERATURE 450°
DISHWASHER-SAFE Yes

COOKING ★★½
EASE OF USE ★
CLEANUP ★
SIZE ★
SAFETY ★

This hulking air fryer, which resembled a salon hair dryer, hogged our counters with its 17-inch footprint. Its heavy flip-top lid needed 2 feet of clearance to open all the way and lock into place—a safety problem since the main heating element was fully exposed when the lid was open. It came with a maddening 11 attachments, many without clear uses (what does one do with a "steak cage"?) or even handles to enable us to remove them from the air fryer when hot. Instead, we had to rely on the laughable "lifter" tool, essentially a flimsy pair of extra-long tweezers.

MAKING THE MOST OF YOUR AIR FRYER

We love the hands-off ease of cooking in an air fryer, but we found that getting the best results involved slightly more than simply turning it on and walking away. The following tricks had big effects on the overall flavor and texture of our food.

More Even Cooking

Avoid overfilling: Air fryers work by circulating hot air around food, but if the food is packed too tightly it will steam instead of crisp and will cook unevenly. (That said, proteins shrink as they cook, so a snug fit with meat is OK.) We took a "jigsaw puzzle" approach to fitting foods, cutting larger proteins in half and skewering smaller pieces to make it easier to arrange more food in the basket without overcrowding.

Rotate and flip meats: It may seem fussy given that the meat is surrounded by hot air, but we found that turning it partway through cooking helped it to cook more evenly.

Toss vegetables: We got more even browning when we tossed vegetables half-way through cooking them. For smaller cuts, such as fries, tossing them in a separate bowl proved to be more efficient; it also allowed us to add sea-sonings such as grated cheese partway through cooking.

Tuck in the tails: When cooking proteins of uneven thick-ness, such as pork tenderloins or fish fillets, we folded the thinner "tails" underneath to create a more uniform size.

"Lincoln-log" 'em: Kebabs are fun to eat and provide an easy way to space out food in the basket. Four or more skewers, when stacked in a perpendicular arrangement (log-cabin style), maximized air exposure. We employed the same method with our Zucchini Fries.

Better Browning

Pat food dry: A dry surface browns more quickly than a wet one, since moisture on the surface will steam, so we patted meats and some vegetables with paper towels before cooking.

A little fat helps: Cooking without any oil whatsoever may sound appealing, but fat promotes browning and can help food to crisp up. In many recipes we found that adding even a small amount of oil gave great results.

Try a little honey: Fat isn't the only way to boost browning. The sugar in honey also browns well in the intense heat of the air fryer and flavors the food as it cooks. (Fruit preserves work too.)

Brush dough with egg wash: When cooking pastry dough in the air fryer, as for our Southwestern Beef Hand Pies (page 84), we found that brushing the tops with egg wash gave us even, glossy browning.

FROM FREEZER TO FRYER!

Because air fryers excel at crisping up small batches of frozen foods (unlike, say, the microwave), we decided to ditch the processed ingredients and create our own from-scratch frozen foods. The following recipes can be made ahead and frozen, then dropped into the air fryer at a moment's notice for an easy weeknight dinner or midnight snack.

- **Better-Than-Boxed Fish Sticks** (page 114)
- **Chicken Nuggets** (page 18)
- **Southwestern Beef Hand Pies** (page 84)

Crunchier Coating

Pretoast your crumbs: Panko bread crumbs, with their coarse, craggy shape, provided the most satisfyingly crunchy coating to most of our air-fried foods. Without any prep the hot air simply dried them out, but a quick pretoast in the microwave with a little oil turned them an irresistible golden brown.

Spray with vegetable oil spray: Lightly spraying the base of the air-fryer basket with vegetable oil spray ensured any crust remained attached to the food.

Juicy Steaks and Roasts

Cut meat down to size: Cutting larger steaks and halving pork tenderloins enabled us to fit more meat into the air fryer without overcrowding.

Add a rub: Steaks and chops emerged juicy and evenly cooked, but their surfaces often needed a flavor and color boost, especially leaner proteins. Adding a potent spice rub gave us better overall color as well as incredible flavor.

Crispy-Skin Chicken

Skin side up: Air fryers heat from above, so we finished cooking skin-on poultry with the skin side up to let it crisp in the direct heat. This meant starting thicker bone-in breasts skin side down and then flipping them, while we cooked thighs and split Cornish game hens skin side up throughout.

Give it a poke: Using a skewer to poke a few holes into fattier chicken thighs and drumsticks helped to render additional fat.

No-Fail Fish

Dial down the temperature: We like air fryers for their intense heat, but some foods, such as fish, needed lower temperatures in order to cook through without the exterior becoming dry. A cooler temperature also gave the crust more time to brown.

Use a foil sling: Delicate fish was prone to sticking and breaking, so a foil sling facilitated easy removal.

Making Complete Meals

Stack your dinner: How do you produce both a main and a side in the air fryer's compact space? Layer them. Placing our protein directly over vegetables not only yielded a full meal but allowed the meat's juices to baste the veggies below.

Use time wisely: Air frying is so hands-off it's easy to focus on preparing a simple side or sauce to go with the main dish. Many of our recipes give suggestions for side dishes that you can make while your protein cooks.

Enlist the microwave: There's no need to turn on the stove when air-frying, but we did find the microwave incredibly helpful in parcooking certain foods, speeding up overall cook time. We also used it to prepare simple sauces to make many of our meals complete.

Smoking or Smell Issues?

Clean your air fryer! We found that the biggest problems with smoking and smell were due to a dirty air fryer. If you see excessive smoke or smell burning even though your food is not burnt, clean the area around the cooled heating element to remove built-up residue. Periodically check for food splatter when the unit isn't in use and clean with mild detergent.

MAKING A FOIL SLING

Fold one long sheet of aluminum foil so it is 4 inches wide. Lay the sheet of foil widthwise across the basket, pressing the foil up and into the sides of the basket. Fold the excess foil as needed so that the edges of the foil are flush with the top of the basket.

SEVEN SIMPLE USES FOR AN AIR FRYER

Roast garlic

Remove outer papery skins from 1 large head garlic. Cut off top third of head to expose cloves and discard. Place garlic head cut side up in center of large piece of aluminum foil, drizzle with ½ teaspoon extra-virgin olive oil, and season with salt. Gather foil tightly around garlic to form packet and place packet in air-fryer basket. Set temperature to 400 degrees, place basket in air fryer, and cook until garlic is soft and golden, about 20 minutes. Carefully open packet to let garlic cool slightly. When cool enough to handle, squeeze cloves from skins; discard skins. Makes about 2 tablespoons.

Roast peppers

Cut ½ inch from top and bottom of up to 3 bell peppers; discard or save for another use. Using paring knife, remove ribs from peppers and discard along with core and seeds. Arrange peppers in air-fryer basket on their sides. (Peppers will fit snugly, but shouldn't come in contact with heating element.) Place basket in air fryer and set temperature to 400 degrees. Cook until peppers have collapsed and skins are browned and wrinkled, about 25 minutes, flipping and rotating peppers halfway through cooking. Transfer peppers to bowl, cover tightly with plastic wrap, and let steam for 10 minutes. Uncover bowl and let peppers cool slightly. When cool enough to handle, peel skin from flesh and discard.

Make croutons

Cut 3 ounces baguette into ¾-inch pieces (you should have 3 cups). Toss bread with 2 tablespoons extra-virgin olive oil, ¼ teaspoon pepper, and ⅛ teaspoon salt in bowl until evenly coated; transfer to air-fryer basket. Place basket in air fryer and set temperature to 350 degrees. Cook, returning croutons to now-empty bowl and tossing to redistribute every 2 minutes until golden and crisp, 6 to 10 minutes. Let croutons cool completely.

Toast nuts and seeds (walnuts, almonds, cashews, pine nuts, pepitas)

While we were able to toast most nuts and seeds in the basket of our winning air fryer, you may find that some smaller nuts and seeds (like sesame seeds and pine nuts) fall through the holes in your basket, as different air-fryer baskets are designed a little differently.

Place up to 1 cup nuts or seeds in air-fryer basket, place basket in air fryer, and set temperature to 350 degrees. Cook, shaking basket occasionally, until nuts or seeds are fragrant, 6 to 10 minutes.

Bake cookies

Depending on the size and shape of your air-fryer basket you may be able to bake more than one cookie at a time.

Make foil sling for air-fryer basket following instructions on page 11. Place 1 frozen or refrigerated cookie dough ball (about 3 tablespoons dough) on sling in prepared basket. Place basket in air fryer and set temperature to 325 degrees. Bake until cookie is golden brown and edges have begun to set but center is still soft and puffy, 10 to 14 minutes.

Make crispy shallots

Toss 4 thinly sliced shallots with ½ teaspoon oil in bowl; transfer to air-fryer basket. Place basket in air fryer and set temperature to 300 degrees. Cook, tossing occasionally, until shallots are golden and crisp, 10 to 12 minutes. Season with salt to taste. Makes about ¾ cup.

Toast burger or sandwich buns

Wipe out air-fryer basket with paper towels after cooking burgers or other food and arrange 2 split buns cut side down in basket. Place basket in air fryer and set temperature to 400 degrees. Cook until lightly golden, 2 to 3 minutes.

CHICKEN AND TURKEY

CHICKEN PARMESAN

Serves 2

COOK TIME 13 minutes   **TOTAL TIME** 45 minutes

why this recipe works Crisp and gooey when done right, but too often oily and soggy, chicken Parmesan seemed an ideal candidate for the air fryer. We could eliminate the greasy pan frying and simplify this multistep dish. But we soon learned that, without a pan of hot oil, the coating of crunchy panko bread crumbs refused to brown. This was easily fixed: Pretoasting the panko in the microwave with a bit of olive oil turned it richly golden. To streamline the breading process, we whisked the flour and egg together, adding garlic powder and dried oregano for flavor. We dipped our chicken in this mixture, then pressed it in the toasted panko that we'd combined with grated Parmesan for an extra hit of cheesiness and an even crunchier texture. A short stint in the air fryer gave us chicken that was juicy inside and crunchy outside—perfect! We sprinkled on shredded mozzarella and cooked the cutlets just long enough to melt the cheese. A little warmed pasta sauce poured over the top kept our recipe simple and avoided soggy cutlets. Chopped basil added a fresh finish. Serve with pasta if desired.

¾ cup panko bread crumbs	¾ teaspoon garlic powder	2 ounces whole-milk mozzarella cheese, shredded (½ cup)
2 tablespoons extra-virgin olive oil	½ teaspoon dried oregano	¼ cup jarred marinara sauce, warmed
¼ cup grated Parmesan cheese	Salt and pepper	2 tablespoons chopped fresh basil
1 large egg	2 (8-ounce) boneless, skinless chicken breasts, trimmed	
1 tablespoon all-purpose flour		

1 Toss panko with oil in bowl until evenly coated. Microwave, stirring frequently, until light golden brown, 1 to 3 minutes. Transfer to shallow dish, let cool slightly, then stir in Parmesan. Whisk egg, flour, garlic powder, oregano, ⅛ teaspoon salt, and ⅛ teaspoon pepper together in second shallow dish.

2 Pound chicken to uniform thickness as needed. Pat dry with paper towels and season with salt and pepper. Working with 1 breast at a time, dredge in egg mixture, letting excess drip off, then coat with panko mixture, pressing gently to adhere.

3 Lightly spray base of air-fryer basket with vegetable oil spray. Arrange breasts in prepared basket, spaced evenly apart, alternating ends. Place basket in air fryer and set temperature to 400 degrees. Cook until chicken is crisp and registers 160 degrees, 12 to 16 minutes, flipping and rotating breasts halfway through cooking.

4 Sprinkle chicken with mozzarella. Return basket to air fryer and cook until cheese is melted, about 1 minute. Transfer chicken to individual serving plates. Top each breast with 2 tablespoons warm marinara sauce and sprinkle with basil. Serve.

CHICKEN NUGGETS

Makes 36 nuggets; serves 4

COOK TIME 12 minutes   **TOTAL TIME** 1 hour, plus freezing time

why this recipe works These homemade nuggets are tender and juicy, not gristly and spongy. And they're convenient if made ahead and frozen, ready to be popped in the air fryer at short notice. A 15-minute brine seasoned the white meat and guarded against dryness even after freezing. Two dipping sauces completed the picture. The air fryer cooks up to 18 nuggets at once; this recipe makes double that, so you'll have plenty on hand. The nuggets can be cooked from fresh without freezing; reduce the cooking time to 10 to 12 minutes, tossing halfway through cooking. Respray the basket before cooking additional batches.

4 (8-ounce) boneless, skinless chicken breasts, trimmed	3 cups panko bread crumbs	3 tablespoons all-purpose flour
Salt and pepper	¼ cup extra-virgin olive oil	1 tablespoon onion powder
3 tablespoons sugar	3 large eggs	¾ teaspoon garlic powder

1 Pound chicken to uniform thickness as needed. Cut each breast diagonally into thirds, then cut each piece into thirds. Dissolve 3 tablespoons salt and sugar in 2 quarts cold water in large container. Add chicken, cover, and let sit for 15 minutes.

2 Meanwhile, toss panko with oil in bowl until evenly coated. Microwave, stirring frequently, until light golden brown, about 5 minutes. Transfer to shallow dish and let cool slightly. Whisk eggs, flour, onion powder, garlic powder, 1 teaspoon salt, and ¼ teaspoon pepper together in second shallow dish.

3 Set wire rack in rimmed baking sheet. Remove chicken from brine and pat dry with paper towels. Working with several chicken pieces at a time, dredge in egg mixture, letting excess drip off, then coat with panko mixture, pressing gently to adhere; transfer to prepared rack. Freeze until firm, about 4 hours. (Frozen nuggets can be transferred to zipper-lock bag and stored in freezer for up to 1 month.)

4 to cook nuggets Lightly spray base of air-fryer basket with vegetable oil spray. Place up to 18 nuggets in prepared basket. Place basket in air fryer, set temperature to 400 degrees, and cook for 6 minutes. Transfer nuggets to clean bowl and gently toss to redistribute. Return nuggets to air fryer and cook until chicken is crisp and registers 160 degrees, 6 to 10 minutes. Serve.

SWEET-AND-SOUR DIPPING SAUCE
Whisk ¾ cup apple jelly, 1 tablespoon distilled white vinegar, ½ teaspoon soy sauce, ⅛ teaspoon garlic powder, pinch ground ginger, and pinch cayenne pepper together in bowl; season with salt and pepper to taste. (Sauce can be refrigerated for up to 4 days; bring to room temperature before serving.)

HONEY-DIJON DIPPING SAUCE
Whisk ½ cup Dijon mustard and ¼ cup honey together in bowl; season with salt and pepper to taste. (Sauce can be refrigerated for up to 4 days; bring to room temperature before serving.)

NUT-CRUSTED CHICKEN BREASTS

Serves 2

COOK TIME 12 minutes   TOTAL TIME 45 minutes

why this recipe works The air fryer excels at simplifying mealtime standbys. Case in point: breaded chicken. No fussy pan frying necessary, and the results are crisp and supremely juicy. Since plain breaded chicken cutlets can be a little boring, we combined panko bread crumbs with finely chopped almonds for a richer, more robust crust, brightening the mix with lemon zest. Pretoasting the coating in a little butter helped it attain a nice golden brown hue; just 2 tablespoons of butter enhanced the almonds' flavor and added even more richness. Pounding the chicken to uniform thickness ensured it would cook evenly in the air fryer's intense heat, and stirring a little flour and seasonings into beaten egg created a "glue" that enabled the nut coating to adhere. Flipping and rotating the chicken once halfway through cooking further guaranteed perfectly cooked cutlets. Fresh lemon wedges cut through the richness of our easy nut-crusted chicken.

½ cup slivered almonds, chopped fine

½ cup panko bread crumbs

2 tablespoons unsalted butter, melted

1 teaspoon grated lemon zest, plus lemon wedges for serving

Salt and pepper

1 large egg

1 tablespoon all-purpose flour

1 teaspoon minced fresh thyme or ½ teaspoon dried

Pinch cayenne pepper

2 (8-ounce) boneless, skinless chicken breasts, trimmed

1 Combine almonds, panko, melted butter, lemon zest, and ¼ teaspoon salt in bowl and microwave, stirring occasionally, until panko is light golden brown and almonds are fragrant, about 4 minutes. Transfer to shallow dish and set aside to cool slightly. Whisk egg, flour, thyme, and cayenne together in second shallow dish.

2 Pound chicken to uniform thickness as needed. Pat dry with paper towels and season with salt and pepper. Working with 1 breast at a time, dredge in egg mixture, letting excess drip off, then coat with panko mixture, pressing gently to adhere.

3 Lightly spray base of air-fryer basket with vegetable oil spray. Arrange breasts in prepared basket, spaced evenly apart, alternating ends. Place basket in air fryer and set temperature to 400 degrees. Cook until chicken is crisp and registers 160 degrees, 12 to 16 minutes, flipping and rotating breasts halfway through cooking. Serve with lemon wedges.

SPICY FRIED-CHICKEN SANDWICH

Serves 4

COOK TIME 12 minutes   **TOTAL TIME** 40 minutes

why this recipe works Crunchy, juicy, and slicked with mayo, a spicy fried chicken sandwich is a lunchtime favorite, but we aren't about to heat up a skillet of frying oil whenever the craving strikes. The air fryer gave us a less greasy route that was nearly as convenient as hitting up our favorite lunch spot. For our spicy chicken sandwich to live up to its name, we added heat in three stages. First, we whisked hot sauce into the egg-flour dredging mixture to ensure the heat was directly coating the chicken rather than getting lost in the breading, as it does in many recipes. Combining more hot sauce with mayonnaise for a creamy spread upped the heat level further. An unwritten rule of fried sandwiches states that a pickled element is a must; this was our opportunity to add even more heat with fiery sweet pickled jalapeños in lieu of pickle chips. Shredded lettuce provided a crisp, fresh component that tempered the heat a bit. You can use your air fryer to toast the buns; see page 13 for more information.

- 1 cup panko bread crumbs
- 2 tablespoons extra-virgin olive oil
- 1 large egg
- 3 tablespoons hot sauce
- 1 tablespoon all-purpose flour
- ½ teaspoon garlic powder
- Salt and pepper
- 2 (8-ounce) boneless, skinless chicken breasts, trimmed
- ¼ cup mayonnaise
- 4 hamburger buns, toasted if desired
- 2 cups shredded iceberg lettuce
- ¼ cup jarred sliced jalapeños

1 Toss panko with oil in bowl until evenly coated. Microwave, stirring frequently, until light golden brown, 1 to 3 minutes. Transfer to shallow dish and set aside to cool slightly. Whisk egg, 2 tablespoons hot sauce, flour, garlic powder, ⅛ teaspoon salt, and ⅛ teaspoon pepper together in second shallow dish.

2 Pound chicken to uniform thickness as needed. Halve each breast crosswise, pat dry with paper towels, and season with salt and pepper. Working with 1 piece of chicken at a time, dredge in egg mixture, letting excess drip off, then coat with panko mixture, pressing gently to adhere.

3 Lightly spray base of air-fryer basket with vegetable oil spray. Arrange chicken pieces in prepared basket, spaced evenly apart. Place basket in air fryer and set temperature to 400 degrees. Cook until chicken is crisp and registers 160 degrees, 12 to 16 minutes, flipping and rotating chicken pieces halfway through cooking.

4 Combine mayonnaise and remaining 1 tablespoon hot sauce in small bowl. Spread mayonnaise mixture evenly over bun bottoms, then top with 1 piece chicken, lettuce, jalapeños, and bun tops. Serve.

APRICOT-THYME GLAZED CHICKEN BREASTS

Serves 2

COOK TIME 12 minutes   **TOTAL TIME** 40 minutes

why this recipe works Glazed boneless chicken breasts are a fast and flavorful addition to anyone's weeknight meal rotation. To make them especially hands-off, we simply placed two breasts, rubbed with oil, in the air fryer and let the hot air work its magic, brushing on the glaze after flipping the chicken to prevent it from sticking to the basket. When it comes to glaze, many recipes invest too much time creating a mixture that just slides off and ends up in the bottom of the pan. For a slightly sweet, no-fuss glaze that stayed put, we reached for one of our favorite fruit condiments: apricot preserves. The chunkier preserves offered a more pleasant texture than jam or jelly, their thick, sticky consistency helped them adhere, and the chunky bits browned up nicely. Just a few seconds in the microwave made the preserves much easier to spread, and a little fresh thyme added a slight woodsy flavor that balanced the apricot's sweet tartness. For a simple variation, we combined the sweetness of pineapple preserves and the warm, spicy bite of fresh ginger.

2 tablespoons apricot preserves	2 (8-ounce) boneless, skinless chicken breasts, trimmed	Salt and pepper
½ teaspoon minced fresh thyme or ⅛ teaspoon dried	1 teaspoon vegetable oil	

1 Microwave apricot preserves and thyme in bowl until fluid, about 30 seconds; set aside. Pound chicken to uniform thickness as needed. Pat dry with paper towels, rub with oil, and season with salt and pepper.

2 Arrange breasts skinned side down in air-fryer basket, spaced evenly apart, alternating ends. Place basket in air fryer, set temperature to 400 degrees, and cook chicken for 4 minutes. Flip and rotate chicken, then brush skinned side with apricot-thyme mixture. Return basket to air fryer and cook until chicken registers 160 degrees, 8 to 12 minutes.

3 Transfer chicken to serving platter, tent loosely with aluminum foil, and let rest for 5 minutes. Serve.

PINEAPPLE-GINGER GLAZED CHICKEN BREASTS
Substitute pineapple preserves for apricot preserves and grated fresh ginger for thyme.

UNSTUFFED CHICKEN BREASTS WITH DIJON MAYONNAISE

Serves 2

COOK TIME 13 minutes   **TOTAL TIME** 40 minutes

why this recipe works For all of the fun of rolled and stuffed chicken—the oozing cheese and savory filling—with none of the fuss, we left our chicken breasts unrolled and layered the "fillings" on the outside. First we wrapped chicken breasts (pounded to even thickness) in slices of ham, overlapping the pieces slightly and securing them with toothpicks. We cooked these savory packages in the air fryer until the ham was crisp and the chicken cooked through, then layered on sliced Swiss cheese, which became a gooey topping after just another minute in the air fryer. Delicious as the result was, tasters felt the dish lacked some of the dinner party flair of the original version, so we combined mayonnaise, Dijon mustard, and a little water to create a quick, velvety smooth sauce to drizzle over the chicken and finished it with a sprinkle of peppery chives. Thinly sliced ham is liable to tear, so for best results use slices that are about ⅛ inch thick. You will need four toothpicks for this recipe.

- 2 (8-ounce) boneless, skinless chicken breasts, trimmed

  Salt and pepper

- 4 thick slices ham (4 ounces)

- 2 slices Swiss cheese (2 ounces)

- 2 tablespoons mayonnaise

- 1 tablespoon Dijon mustard

- 1 teaspoon water

- 1 tablespoon minced fresh chives

1 Pound chicken to uniform thickness as needed Pat dry with paper towels and season with salt and pepper. For each chicken breast, shingle 2 slices of ham on counter, overlapping edges slightly, and lay chicken, skinned side down, in center. Fold ham around chicken and secure overlapping ends by threading toothpick through ham and chicken. Flip chicken and thread toothpick through ham and chicken on second side.

2 Lightly spray base of air-fryer basket with vegetable oil spray. Arrange breasts skinned side down in prepared basket, spaced evenly apart, alternating ends. Place basket in air fryer and set temperature to 400 degrees. Cook until edges of ham begin to brown and chicken registers 160 degrees, 12 to 16 minutes, flipping and rotating breasts halfway through cooking. Top each breast with 1 slice Swiss, folding cheese as needed. Return basket to air fryer and cook until cheese is melted, about 1 minute.

3 Transfer chicken to serving platter and discard toothpicks. Tent loosely with aluminum foil and let rest for 5 minutes. Meanwhile, combine mayonnaise, mustard, and water in small bowl. Drizzle chicken with 1 tablespoon sauce and sprinkle with chives. Serve, passing remaining sauce separately.

SPICED CHICKEN BREASTS WITH ASPARAGUS, ARUGULA, AND CANNELLINI BEAN SALAD

Serves 2

COOK TIME 20 minutes   **TOTAL TIME** 45 minutes

why this recipe works Boneless chicken breasts cook so quickly in the air fryer that we wondered, why stop there? Here, we used it to produce a complete meal by cooking chicken and vegetables in stages. We first softened red onion right in the basket, then added asparagus. When the vegetables became tender we stirred them into warmed cannellini beans tossed with a simple dressing. We let that marinate briefly while we air-fried chicken breasts that we had jazzed up with coriander (for its citrus notes) and paprika (for depth). A little baby arugula turned our vegetables and beans into a salad. Rinsing the cannellini beans eliminates any slimy texture. Look for asparagus spears no thicker than ½ inch.

1   cup canned cannellini beans, rinsed

2   tablespoons extra-virgin olive oil

1½   tablespoons red wine vinegar

1   garlic clove, minced

Salt and pepper

½   red onion, sliced thin

8   ounces asparagus, trimmed and cut into 1-inch lengths

½   teaspoon ground coriander

¼   teaspoon paprika

2   (8-ounce) boneless, skinless chicken breasts, trimmed

2   ounces (2 cups) baby arugula

1 Microwave beans in large bowl until just warm, about 30 seconds. Stir in 1 tablespoon oil, vinegar, garlic, ¼ teaspoon salt, and pinch pepper; set aside.

2 Toss onion with 2 teaspoons oil, ⅛ teaspoon salt, and pinch pepper in clean bowl to coat. Place onion in air-fryer basket, set temperature to 400 degrees, and cook for 2 minutes. Stir in asparagus, return basket to air fryer, and cook until asparagus is tender and bright green, 6 to 8 minutes, tossing halfway through cooking. Transfer to bowl with beans and set aside.

3 Combine coriander, paprika, ¼ teaspoon salt, and ⅛ teaspoon pepper in small bowl. Pound chicken to uniform thickness as needed. Pat dry with paper towels, rub with remaining 1 teaspoon oil, and sprinkle evenly with spice mixture. Arrange breasts skinned side down in now-empty air-fryer basket, spaced evenly apart, alternating ends. Place basket in air fryer and set temperature to 400 degrees. Cook until chicken registers 160 degrees, 12 to 16 minutes, flipping and rotating breasts halfway through cooking.

4 Transfer chicken to serving platter, tent loosely with aluminum foil, and let rest for 5 minutes. Add arugula to asparagus mixture in bowl and toss to combine. Season with salt and pepper to taste. Serve chicken with salad.

ROASTED BONE-IN CHICKEN BREASTS

Serves 2

COOK TIME 20 minutes   **TOTAL TIME** 30 minutes

why this recipe works When it's just two of you, roasting a whole chicken can feel like far too much trouble for a busy night. But roasting a pair of bone-in chicken breasts in the air fryer is a snap, and there are no leftovers to deal with. Bone-in chicken cooks beautifully in the air fryer, and the circulated hot air does nearly all the work. We rubbed the breasts with just a teaspoon of oil to ensure crispy skin and flipped and rotated them halfway through cooking, starting them skin side down to help the fat in the skin to render, then flipping them so the skin could brown. A moderate 350 degrees minimized moisture loss and resulted in perfectly juicy meat. For a sauce to drizzle over our roasted breasts, we created two bright, fresh options, either of which can be prepared while the chicken cooks (one enlists the micro-wave but neither requires a pan or even a blender, keeping the prep minimal and cutting down on dishes to wash). With our chicken roasted, all that remained was to toss a simple salad, perhaps open a bottle of wine, and *voilà*—a fancy dinner for two ready in 30 minutes! For an elegant presentation, cut the chicken breasts off the bone before serving.

2 (12-ounce) bone-in split chicken breasts, trimmed	1 teaspoon extra-virgin olive oil	Salt and pepper

Pat chicken dry with paper towels, rub with oil, and season with salt and pepper. Arrange breasts skin side down in air-fryer basket, spaced evenly apart, alternating ends. Place basket in air fryer and set temperature to 350 degrees. Cook until chicken registers 160 degrees, 20 to 25 minutes, flipping and rotating breasts halfway through cooking. Transfer chicken to serving platter, tent loosely with aluminum foil, and let rest for 5 minutes. Serve.

PEACH-GINGER CHUTNEY
Microwave 1 teaspoon extra-virgin olive oil, 1 small minced shallot, 1 minced garlic clove, 1 teaspoon grated fresh ginger, ⅛ teaspoon salt, and pinch red pepper flakes in medium bowl until shallot has softened, about 1 minute.

Stir in 1½ cups frozen peaches, thawed and cut into ½-inch pieces; 2 tablespoons packed light brown sugar; and 1½ tablespoons cider vinegar. Microwave until peaches have softened and liquid is thick and syrupy, 6 to 8 minutes, stirring occasionally. Stir in 1 tablespoon chopped crystallized ginger.

LEMON-BASIL SALSA VERDE
Whisk ¼ cup minced fresh parsley, ¼ cup chopped fresh basil, 3 tablespoons extra-virgin olive oil, 1 tablespoon rinsed and minced capers, 1 tablespoon water, 2 minced garlic cloves, 1 rinsed and minced anchovy fillet, ½ teaspoon grated lemon zest and 2 teaspoons juice, and ⅛ teaspoon salt together in bowl.

ROASTED BONE-IN CHICKEN BREASTS AND FINGERLING POTATOES WITH SUN-DRIED TOMATO RELISH

Serves 2

COOK TIME 20 minutes   **TOTAL TIME** 40 minutes

why this recipe works One of our favorite ways to roast chicken is on a pile of potatoes, which become flavored by the chicken's savory drippings as they roast. Moving the process to the air fryer gave us crispier, less greasy results, as the circulated hot air cooked the potatoes from all sides, while the wire basket allowed excess fat to drip below. We filled the basket with quick-cooking fingerling potatoes tossed with garlic, oil, and herbs. Above this, we placed two bone-in chicken breasts—rubbed with more oil and herbs. We started the chicken skin side down to render drippings, which seasoned the potatoes, then flipped it to allow the skin to crisp. Afterward, we collected a small spoonful of drippings from the bottom of the air fryer and used it to flavor a sun-dried tomato relish, which brought savory depth to our meal. Look for fingerling potatoes about 3 inches in length.

- 1 pound fingerling potatoes, unpeeled
- 2 teaspoons extra-virgin olive oil, plus extra as needed
- 2 teaspoons minced fresh thyme or ¾ teaspoon dried
- 2 teaspoons minced fresh oregano or ¾ teaspoon dried
- 1 garlic clove, minced

  Salt and pepper
- 2 (12-ounce) bone-in split chicken breasts, trimmed
- ¼ cup oil-packed sun-dried tomatoes, patted dry and chopped fine
- 1 small shallot, minced
- 1½ tablespoons red wine vinegar
- 1 tablespoon capers, rinsed and minced

1 Toss potatoes with 1 teaspoon oil, 1 teaspoon thyme, 1 teaspoon oregano, garlic, ¼ teaspoon salt, and ¼ teaspoon pepper in bowl to coat; transfer to air-fryer basket.

2 Pat chicken dry with paper towels. Rub with remaining 1 teaspoon oil, season with salt and pepper, and sprinkle with remaining 1 teaspoon thyme and 1 teaspoon oregano. Arrange breasts skin side down on top of potatoes, spaced evenly apart, alternating ends. Place basket in air fryer and set temperature to 350 degrees. Cook until potatoes are tender and chicken registers 160 degrees, 20 to 25 minutes, flipping and rotating breasts halfway through cooking.

3 Transfer chicken and potatoes to serving platter, tent loosely with aluminum foil, and let rest for 5 minutes. Pour off and reserve 1½ tablespoons juices from air-fryer drawer (add extra oil as needed to equal 1½ tablespoons). Combine tomatoes, shallot, vinegar, capers, ⅛ teaspoon salt, ⅛ teaspoon pepper, and reserved chicken juices in bowl. Serve chicken and potatoes with tomato relish.

BARBECUED BONE-IN CHICKEN BREASTS WITH CREAMY COLESLAW

Serves 2

COOK TIME 20 minutes   **TOTAL TIME** 45 minutes

why this recipe works Barbecued bone-in chicken on the grill can be tricky, what with flare-ups and unevenly cooked meat. For an easier indoor take, the air fryer stood in admirably, allowing us to cook the chicken nearly unattended. We used two bone-in chicken breasts and started cooking them skin side down to avoid drying them out. For plenty of barbecue flavor, we flipped the chicken and brushed the skin with a generous amount of barbecue sauce, finishing the cooking skin side up so the sauce could caramelize a bit in the air fryer's circulated heat. For a convenient slaw that held its own, we started with bagged coleslaw mix. Salting the cabbage mixture for 30 minutes drew out excess moisture, avoiding a watery slaw, and softened the vegetables. For a dressing, we cut the standard mayonnaise with an equal amount of sour cream, which improved the texture and added richness and tang. White vinegar and a small amount of sugar gave the dressing balance.

3   cups (8 ounces) shredded coleslaw mix

Salt and pepper

2   (12-ounce) bone-in split chicken breasts, trimmed

1   teaspoon vegetable oil

2   tablespoons barbecue sauce, plus extra for serving

2   tablespoons mayonnaise

2   tablespoons sour cream

1   teaspoon distilled white vinegar, plus extra for seasoning

¼   teaspoon sugar

1 Toss coleslaw mix and ¼ teaspoon salt in colander set over bowl. Let sit until wilted slightly, about 30 minutes. Rinse, drain, and dry well with dish towel.

2 Meanwhile, pat chicken dry with paper towels, rub with oil, and season with salt and pepper. Arrange breasts skin side down in air-fryer basket, spaced evenly apart, alternating ends. Place basket in air fryer, set temperature to 350 degrees, and cook for 10 minutes. Flip and rotate breasts, then brush skin side with barbecue sauce. Return basket to air fryer and cook until well browned and chicken registers 160 degrees, 10 to 15 minutes.

3 Transfer chicken to serving platter, tent loosely with aluminum foil, and let rest for 5 minutes. While chicken rests, whisk mayonnaise, sour cream, vinegar, sugar, and pinch pepper together in large bowl. Stir in coleslaw mix and season with salt, pepper, and additional vinegar to taste. Serve chicken with coleslaw, passing extra barbecue sauce separately.

POMEGRANATE-GLAZED BONE-IN CHICKEN BREASTS WITH COUSCOUS SALAD

Serves 2

COOK TIME 20 minutes   **TOTAL TIME** 50 minutes

why this recipe works For intensely flavored glazed chicken, rather than reach for an armful of ingredients, we turned to sweet-tart pomegranate molasses, a Mediterranean staple. Glazing the skin with pomegranate molasses in two applications not only brought sweet, sour, and fruity notes but produced richly burnished skin. Cinnamon and thyme complemented the glaze. For a quick side, we prepared a Mediterranean couscous salad tossed in a simple pomegranate vinaigrette. Dressing the couscous while still warm helped it to absorb more of the dressing. Cherry tomatoes, scallion, feta, and parsley gave the salad bright and contrasting flavors. You can find pomegranate molasses in the international aisle of well-stocked supermarkets.

3 tablespoons plus 2 teaspoons pomegranate molasses

1 teaspoon minced fresh thyme

½ teaspoon ground cinnamon

Salt and pepper

2 (12-ounce) bone-in split chicken breasts, trimmed

2 tablespoons extra-virgin olive oil

¼ cup water

¼ cup chicken broth

½ cup couscous

1 scallion, white part minced, green part sliced thin on bias

2 ounces cherry tomatoes, quartered

1 tablespoon minced fresh parsley

1 ounce feta cheese, crumbled (¼ cup)

1 Combine 3 tablespoons pomegranate molasses, thyme, cinnamon, and ⅛ teaspoon salt in small bowl. Pat chicken dry with paper towels, rub with 1 teaspoon oil, and season with salt and pepper. Arrange breasts skin side down in air-fryer basket, spaced evenly apart, alternating ends. Place basket in air fryer, set temperature to 350 degrees, and cook for 10 minutes.

2 Flip and rotate breasts, then brush skin with half of pomegranate molasses mixture. Return basket to air fryer and cook for 5 minutes. Brush breasts with remaining pomegranate molasses mixture, return basket to air fryer, and continue to cook until well browned and chicken registers 160 degrees, 5 to 10 minutes. Transfer chicken to serving platter, tent loosely with aluminum foil, and let rest for 5 minutes.

3 Meanwhile, microwave water and broth in medium bowl until very hot, 3 to 5 minutes. Stir in couscous and ⅛ teaspoon salt. Cover and let sit until couscous is tender and all liquid has been absorbed, about 7 minutes.

4 Whisk remaining 5 teaspoons oil, remaining 2 teaspoons pomegranate molasses, and scallion whites together in clean bowl. Add tomatoes, parsley, scallion greens, and pomegranate-oil mixture to couscous and gently fluff with fork to combine. Sprinkle with feta and serve with chicken.

AIR-FRIED CHICKEN

Serves 2

COOK TIME 16 minutes   **TOTAL TIME** 50 minutes

why this recipe works Our air-fried chicken comes out golden and crispy on the outside and moist and juicy on the inside, and needs only a light spray of vegetable oil to become crisp. The secret was removing the fatty skin and finding a coating that would become crunchy without needing to be fried in a pan of hot oil. In a side-by-side taste test, crushed cornflakes won out over bread crumbs and Melba toast, offering the best color and crispness, but the results tasted a bit like breakfast cereal. Spicing up the cornflakes with poultry seasoning, paprika, and cayenne pepper gave the coating the savory element it needed. Dredging the floured chicken pieces in buttermilk added tang and ensured the crumbs stuck to the chicken. To crush the cornflakes, place them inside a zipper-lock bag and use a rolling pin or the bottom of a large skillet to break them into fine crumbs. To help remove the skin from the chicken, use a paper towel to grasp the skin. If you prefer, you can use a combination of two 5-ounce thighs and two 5-ounce drumsticks instead of the chicken breasts; if using drumsticks and thighs, be sure to cook them until they register 175 degrees, 20 to 25 minutes.

Vegetable oil spray

2 (12-ounce) bone-in split chicken breasts, trimmed

Salt and pepper

⅓ cup buttermilk

½ teaspoon dry mustard

½ teaspoon garlic powder

¼ cup all-purpose flour

2 cups (2 ounces) cornflakes, finely crushed

1½ teaspoons poultry seasoning

½ teaspoon paprika

⅛ teaspoon cayenne pepper

1 Lightly spray base of air-fryer basket with oil spray. Remove skin from chicken and trim any excess fat. Halve each breast crosswise, pat dry with paper towels, and season with salt and pepper. Whisk buttermilk, mustard, garlic powder, ½ teaspoon salt, and ¼ teaspoon pepper together in medium bowl. Spread flour in shallow dish. Combine cornflakes, poultry seasoning, paprika, ¼ teaspoon salt, and cayenne in second shallow dish.

2 Working with 1 piece of chicken at a time, dredge in flour, dip in buttermilk mixture, letting excess drip off, then coat with cornflake mixture, pressing gently to adhere; transfer to large plate. Lightly spray chicken with oil spray.

3 Arrange chicken pieces in prepared basket, spaced evenly apart. Place basket in air fryer and set temperature to 400 degrees. Cook until chicken is crisp and registers 160 degrees, 16 to 24 minutes, flipping and rotating pieces halfway through cooking. Serve.

THAI CORNISH GAME HENS WITH CUCUMBER SALAD

Serves 2

COOK TIME 23 minutes   **TOTAL TIME** 1 hour

why this recipe works Cornish game hens are ideally suited to the air fryer: The quick-cooking birds crisp up beautifully, offering a special meal with little effort. For hens that were bursting with flavor, we were inspired by Thai grilled chicken (*gai yang*), a ubiquitous street food featuring a pungent salty-sweet marinade that despite its exotic flavor can be assembled with relatively common ingredients. We first tried air-frying two small whole game hens; they just fit, but butterflying and halving them allowed for a faster cook time. We rubbed a thick aromatic marinade of cilantro, fish sauce, sugar, garlic, lime zest, black pepper, and coriander under the skin and let the birds sit; 10 minutes was enough to infuse them with flavor. Poking holes in the skin helped the fat to render and aided crisping. To ensure even cooking, we rotated the split hens when they were halfway done, but kept them skin side up, which yielded beautifully browned skin. While the hens rested, we assembled a refreshing cucumber salad dressed with lime juice, fish sauce, sugar, and a Thai chile—hitting the mix of sour, salty, sweet, and spicy flavor that makes Thai food so unique and irresistible. If you can't find a Thai chile, you can substitute a Fresno or red jalapeño chile.

- 2 (1¼-pound) Cornish game hens, giblets discarded
- 6 tablespoons chopped fresh cilantro
- 2 tablespoons packed light brown sugar
- 1 tablespoon fish sauce
- 2 garlic cloves, minced
- 2 teaspoons grated lime zest plus 1 tablespoon juice, plus lime wedges for serving
- 2 teaspoons vegetable oil
- 1 teaspoon ground coriander

  Salt and pepper
- 1 Thai chile, stemmed, seeded, and minced
- 1 English cucumber, halved lengthwise and sliced thin
- 1 small shallot, sliced thin
- 2 tablespoons chopped dry-roasted peanuts

1 Lightly spray air-fryer basket with vegetable oil spray. Working with 1 hen at a time, use kitchen shears to cut along both sides of backbone to remove it. Flatten hens and lay breast side up on counter. Using sharp chef's knife, cut through center of breast to make 2 halves.

2 Using your fingers, gently loosen skin covering breast and thighs. Pat hens dry with paper towels. Using metal skewer, poke 10 to 15 holes in fat deposits on top of breasts and thighs. Tuck wingtips underneath hens.

3 Combine ¼ cup cilantro, 4 teaspoons sugar, 2 teaspoons fish sauce, garlic, lime zest, 1 teaspoon oil, coriander, ½ teaspoon pepper, and ⅛ teaspoon salt in bowl. Rub cilantro mixture evenly under skin of hens and set aside to marinate for 10 minutes.

4 Arrange hens breast side up in prepared basket. Place basket in air fryer and set temperature to 400 degrees. Cook until skin is golden and breasts register 160 degrees and thighs register 175 degrees, 23 to 28 minutes, rotating hens halfway through cooking (do not flip). Transfer hens to cutting board, tent loosely with aluminum foil, and let rest for 5 minutes.

5 Meanwhile, whisk lime juice, Thai chile, remaining 2 teaspoons sugar, remaining 1 teaspoon fish sauce, and remaining 1 teaspoon oil together in medium serving bowl. Add cucumber, shallot, and remaining 2 tablespoons cilantro and toss to coat. Season with salt and pepper to taste and sprinkle with peanuts. Serve hens with cucumber salad and lime wedges.

TERIYAKI CHICKEN WITH SNOW PEAS

Serves 2

COOK TIME 27 minutes   **TOTAL TIME** 1 hour

why this recipe works Teriyaki chicken is often grilled or broiled, but the air fryer offered a more fuss-free route to juicy meat and crispy skin slathered with a sweet-salty glaze. To build flavor, we briefly marinated bone-in chicken thighs in a mixture of chicken broth, soy sauce, fresh ginger, and red pepper flakes. Poking holes in the skin helped the marinade penetrate and later helped the skin to crisp. We then combined some of the marinade with sugar, mirin, and cornstarch to produce a balanced (not cloying) teriyaki sauce. We microwaved the sauce to thicken it and brushed it on the chicken before the last 5 minutes of cooking, after the skin had crisped up. While the chicken rested, we used our air fryer to prepare a vegetable "stir-fry" of snow peas tossed with some of the rendered chicken fat, garlic, and lemon zest and juice for brightness.

- ¼ cup chicken broth
- 1½ tablespoons soy sauce
- ½ teaspoon grated fresh ginger
- ⅛ teaspoon red pepper flakes

- 4 (5-ounce) bone-in chicken thighs, trimmed
- 1 tablespoon sugar
- 1 tablespoon mirin
- ½ teaspoon cornstarch
- 6 ounces snow peas, strings removed

- 1 garlic clove, minced
- ⅛ teaspoon grated lemon zest plus ½ teaspoon juice
- ¼ teaspoon salt
- Pinch pepper

1 Whisk broth, soy sauce, ginger, and pepper flakes together in large bowl. Pat chicken dry with paper towels. Using metal skewer, poke skin side of chicken 10 to 15 times. Add to bowl with broth mixture and toss to coat; set aside to marinate for 10 minutes.

2 Remove chicken from marinade and pat dry with paper towels. Measure out 2 tablespoons remaining marinade and combine with sugar, mirin, and cornstarch in bowl; discard remainder. Microwave, stirring occasionally, until thickened and bubbling, about 1 minute; set aside.

3 Arrange chicken skin side up in air-fryer basket, spaced evenly apart. Place basket in air fryer and set temperature to 400 degrees. Cook until chicken is golden, crisp, and registers 195 degrees, 20 to 25 minutes, rotating chicken halfway through cooking (do not flip). Brush chicken skin with thickened marinade mixture. Return basket to air fryer and cook until chicken is well browned, about 5 minutes. Transfer chicken to serving platter, tent with aluminum foil, and let rest for 5 minutes. Measure out ½ teaspoon fat from air-fryer drawer; discard remainder.

4 While chicken rests, toss reserved fat, snow peas, garlic, lemon zest, salt, and pepper together in bowl and transfer to now-empty basket. Place basket in air fryer and cook until snow peas are crisp-tender, 2 to 3 minutes. Transfer to serving bowl and toss with lemon juice. Serve with chicken.

TANDOORI CHICKEN THIGHS

Serves 2

COOK TIME 20 minutes   **TOTAL TIME** 55 minutes

why this recipe works Tandoori chicken traditionally features bone-in pieces marinated in yogurt and spices and cooked in a superhot tandoor clay oven until tender and lightly charred. Most home approximations remain involved affairs with multiple cooking stages. But we found the air fryer worked well at producing great-tasting tandoori in fewer steps. Bone-in chicken thighs gave us moist, rich meat and kept the process simple. To create authentic flavor, we mixed up a spiced yogurt marinade that incorporated garlic, fresh ginger, garam marsala, cumin, and chili powder. Blooming the seasonings first in the microwave released their flavors and tamed the garlic's raw edge. Poking holes in the chicken skin allowed the marinade to penetrate more deeply and helped render fat, and keeping the thighs skin side up throughout cooking developed some nice charring. To complement the chicken, we combined more yogurt with lime juice for a simple, cooling sauce. We prefer this dish with whole-milk yogurt, but low-fat yogurt can be substituted.

- 3 **garlic cloves, minced**
- 1 **tablespoon grated fresh ginger**
- 1½ **teaspoons garam masala**
- 1 **teaspoon ground cumin**
- 1 **teaspoon chili powder**
- 1 **teaspoon vegetable oil**
- **Salt and pepper**
- ½ **cup plain whole-milk yogurt**
- 4 **teaspoons lime juice**
- 4 **(5-ounce) bone-in chicken thighs, trimmed**

1 Combine garlic, ginger, garam masala, cumin, chili powder, oil, ¼ teaspoon salt, and ¼ teaspoon pepper in large bowl and microwave until fragrant, about 30 seconds. Set aside to cool slightly, then stir in ¼ cup yogurt and 1 tablespoon lime juice.

2 Pat chicken dry with paper towels. Using metal skewer, poke skin side of chicken 10 to 15 times. Add to bowl with yogurt-spice mixture and toss to coat; set aside to marinate for 10 minutes. Meanwhile, combine remaining ¼ cup yogurt and remaining 1 teaspoon lime juice in clean bowl; season with salt and pepper to taste and set aside.

3 Remove chicken from marinade, letting excess drip off, and arrange skin side up in air-fryer basket, spaced evenly apart. Place basket in air fryer and set temperature to 400 degrees. Cook until chicken is well browned and crisp and registers 195 degrees, 20 to 30 minutes, rotating chicken halfway through cooking (do not flip).

4 Transfer chicken to serving platter, tent loosely with aluminum foil, and let rest for 5 minutes. Serve with reserved yogurt-lime sauce.

SHREDDED CHICKEN TACOS

Serves 2 to 4

COOK TIME 12 minutes   **TOTAL TIME** 40 minutes

why this recipe works The perfect weeknight chicken tacos should be the kind of no-brainer meal you can comfortably turn to again and again. But often this means wet, oversimmered chicken and tired ingredients. The air fryer gave us something better: crispier, more deeply seasoned chicken, and extra downtime to prepare lively, fresh toppings. Our first step was to skip past the expected boneless chicken breasts in favor of boneless thighs, which are equally convenient but richer and more deeply flavored. Rubbed with just a teaspoon of oil and sprinkled with a robust blend of chili powder, cumin, garlic powder, salt, pepper, and cayenne, they went into the air fryer to cook while we prepared a fresh pico de gallo from chopped tomato, red onion, minced jalapeño, and lime juice. Letting the cooked chicken rest for a few minutes before shredding it ensured the juices remained in the meat and didn't wind up all over the cutting board. Crisp iceberg lettuce and shredded cheddar gave that familiar taco bar feel.

1 teaspoon chili powder	1 pound boneless, skinless chicken thighs, trimmed	2 teaspoons minced jalapeño chile
½ teaspoon ground cumin	1 teaspoon vegetable oil	1½ teaspoons lime juice
½ teaspoon garlic powder	1 tomato, cored and chopped	6–12 (6-inch) corn tortillas, warmed
Salt and pepper	2 tablespoons finely chopped red onion	1 cup shredded iceberg lettuce
Pinch cayenne pepper		3 ounces cheddar cheese, shredded (¾ cup)

1 Combine chili powder, cumin, garlic powder, ½ teaspoon salt, ¼ teaspoon pepper, and cayenne in bowl. Pat chicken dry with paper towels, rub with oil, and sprinkle evenly with spice mixture. Place chicken in air-fryer basket. Place basket in air fryer and set temperature to 400 degrees. Cook until chicken registers 175 degrees, 12 to 16 minutes, flipping and rotating chicken halfway through cooking.

2 Meanwhile, combine tomato, onion, jalapeño, and lime juice in bowl; season with salt and pepper to taste and set aside until ready to serve.

3 Transfer chicken to cutting board, let cool slightly, then shred into bite-size pieces using 2 forks. Serve chicken on warm tortillas, topped with salsa, lettuce, and cheddar.

THAI-STYLE CHICKEN LETTUCE WRAPS

Serves 2 to 4

COOK TIME 12 minutes   **TOTAL TIME** 40 minutes

why this recipe works Based on a light yet bold Thai salad known as *larb*, these chicken lettuce wraps embody the cuisine's signature balance of sweet, sour, salty, and hot flavors. But even the most flavorful salad can't compensate for dry chicken. Choosing boneless chicken thighs ensured the meat would be moist. The air fryer made quick work of cooking the chicken while we mixed a pungent dressing from lime juice, fish sauce, brown sugar, shallot, garlic, and pepper flakes. We let the chicken cool slightly and then shredded it; this subtle but significant step created loads of surface area that allowed the dressing to soak into the meat, ensuring every bite would be saturated with flavor. Fresh herbs (mint, cilantro, and Thai basil), mango, and Thai chiles brought more freshness to our salad, which we spooned into Bibb lettuce cups and sprinkled with chopped peanuts for crunch. If you can't find Thai basil, you can substitute regular basil. If you can't find Thai chiles, you can substitute two Fresno or red jalapeño chiles.

1 pound boneless, skinless chicken thighs, trimmed	2 teaspoons packed brown sugar	⅓ cup chopped fresh cilantro
1 teaspoon vegetable oil	1 garlic clove, minced	⅓ cup chopped fresh Thai basil
2 tablespoons lime juice	⅛ teaspoon red pepper flakes	1 head Bibb lettuce (8 ounces), leaves separated
1 shallot, minced	1 mango, peeled, pitted, and cut into ¼-inch pieces	¼ cup dry-roasted peanuts, chopped
1 tablespoon fish sauce, plus extra for serving	⅓ cup chopped fresh mint	2 Thai chiles, stemmed and sliced thin

1 Pat chicken dry with paper towels and rub with oil. Place chicken in air-fryer basket. Place basket in air fryer and set temperature to 400 degrees. Cook until chicken registers 175 degrees, 12 to 16 minutes, flipping and rotating chicken halfway through cooking.

2 Meanwhile, whisk lime juice, shallot, fish sauce, sugar, garlic, and pepper flakes together in large bowl; set aside.

3 Transfer chicken to cutting board, let cool slightly, then shred into bite-size pieces using 2 forks. Add shredded chicken, mango, mint, cilantro, and basil to bowl with dressing and toss to coat. Serve chicken in lettuce leaves, passing peanuts, Thai chiles, and extra fish sauce separately.

JERK CHICKEN LEG QUARTERS

Serves 2

COOK TIME 27 minutes   **TOTAL TIME** 50 minutes

why this recipe works Spicy, sweet, and herbal, this simple take on Jamaican jerk chicken delivers authentic flavors from a spice rub composed of easily available pantry ingredients. We substituted black pepper, dry mustard, and cayenne pepper for the heat of the usual Scotch bonnet peppers, which can be hard to come by. Ground allspice was key, and dried thyme rounded out the traditional seasonings while brown sugar sweetened things up and helped to create a deep brown, crackly, and crusted skin on our chicken. We chose skin-on chicken leg quarters, a cut that's forgiving to cook and tender down to the last nibble on the bone. It also offered lots of surface area for our jerk rub. To get both tender meat and crispy skin using our air fryer, we pierced the skin in several places to allow the fat underneath to render more quickly, and kept the leg quarters skin side up throughout, ensuring they had time to become deeply colored. Served with lime wedges and a sprinkling of scallion, our jerk chicken legs were mouthwatering; all that was missing was a warm Caribbean breeze. Some leg quarters are sold with the backbone attached. Be sure to remove it (we like to use a heavy chef's knife for this task) before cooking so that the chicken fits in the air-fryer basket and to make serving easier.

1 tablespoon packed brown sugar	¾ teaspoon dry mustard	2 (10-ounce) chicken leg quarters, trimmed
1 teaspoon ground allspice	¾ teaspoon dried thyme	1 teaspoon vegetable oil
1 teaspoon pepper	½ teaspoon salt	1 scallion, green part only, sliced thin
1 teaspoon garlic powder	¼ teaspoon cayenne pepper	Lime wedges

1 Combine sugar, allspice, pepper, garlic powder, mustard, thyme, salt, and cayenne in bowl. Pat chicken dry with paper towels. Using metal skewer, poke 10 to 15 holes in skin of each chicken leg. Rub with oil and sprinkle evenly with spice mixture.

2 Arrange chicken skin side up in air-fryer basket, spaced evenly apart. Place basket in air fryer and set temperature to 400 degrees. Cook until chicken is well browned and crisp and registers 195 degrees, 27 to 30 minutes, rotating chicken halfway through cooking (do not flip).

3 Transfer chicken to plate, tent loosely with aluminum foil, and let rest for 5 minutes. Sprinkle with scallion. Serve with lime wedges.

PAPRIKA-RUBBED CHICKEN DRUMSTICKS

Serves 2

COOK TIME 22 minutes   **TOTAL TIME** 45 minutes

why this recipe works If you know how to do them justice, often-neglected chicken drumsticks can be a standout choice, with tender meat and loads of crispy skin. Their irregular shape and small size make them perfectly suited to cooking in the air fryer, which envelops them in circulated hot air. We wanted a simple recipe for drumsticks that would yield succulent meat perfumed with spices and featuring crisp mahogany skin. Paprika, garlic powder, and dry mustard created the base, while a little brown sugar added sweetness and helped create a slightly glazed exterior on the chicken as it melted. We poked holes in the drumsticks' skin to better render the fat, rubbed on a little oil to help achieve maximum crispness, and sprinkled on our spice rub. In less than 25 minutes we had perfectly cooked drumsticks. Scallion sprinkled over the top just before serving provided an earthy flavor and delicate, fresh crunch.

2 teaspoons paprika	½ teaspoon dry mustard	1 teaspoon vegetable oil
1 teaspoon packed brown sugar	½ teaspoon salt	
	Pinch pepper	1 scallion, green part only, sliced thin on bias
1 teaspoon garlic powder	4 (5-ounce) chicken drumsticks, trimmed	

1 Combine paprika, sugar, garlic powder, mustard, salt, and pepper in bowl. Pat drumsticks dry with paper towels. Using metal skewer, poke 10 to 15 holes in skin of each drumstick. Rub with oil and sprinkle evenly with spice mixture.

2 Arrange drumsticks in air-fryer basket, spaced evenly apart, alternating ends. Place basket in air fryer and set temperature to 400 degrees. Cook until chicken is crisp and registers 195 degrees, 22 to 25 minutes, flipping and rotating chicken halfway through cooking.

3 Transfer chicken to serving platter, tent loosely with aluminum foil, and let rest for 5 minutes. Sprinkle with scallion. Serve.

BUFFALO CHICKEN DRUMSTICKS

Serves 2

COOK TIME 22 minutes   **TOTAL TIME** 45 minutes

why this recipe works An air fryer produces great Buffalo chicken with the crunch that typically comes from deep frying. The catch is that, for well-crisped pieces, you must cook wings in batches—even for two servings—which didn't thrill us. To avoid this, we opted for more substantial drumsticks, turning the snack into a main dish, and found we liked the meatier pieces (still with plenty of crispy skin) prepared Buffalo style. We poked holes in the skin to render the fat efficiently and rubbed them with a touch of oil to ensure they crisped up. To build flavor, we coated the drumsticks with a blend of paprika, cayenne, salt, and pepper before cooking. For the namesake sauce, we microwaved equal parts melted butter and hot sauce but found the coating to be greasy. Using less butter fixed that problem but did not keep the sauce from sliding off the chicken. Adding just ¼ teaspoon of cornstarch yielded a thicker, glazy sauce that coated the drumsticks perfectly, and a bit of molasses deepened its flavor and brought a hint of sweetness. Instead of preparing a blue cheese sauce, we simply crumbled blue cheese over the drumsticks, which balanced the Buffalo sauce's addictive heat. Classic Buffalo sauce is made with Frank's RedHot Original Cayenne Pepper Sauce.

1½ teaspoons paprika	4 (5-ounce) chicken drumsticks, trimmed	2 tablespoons unsalted butter
½ teaspoon cayenne pepper	1 teaspoon vegetable oil	2 teaspoons molasses
¼ teaspoon salt	3 tablespoons hot sauce	¼ teaspoon cornstarch
¼ teaspoon pepper		2 tablespoons crumbled blue cheese

1 Combine paprika, cayenne, salt, and pepper in bowl. Pat drumsticks dry with paper towels. Using metal skewer, poke 10 to 15 holes in skin of each drumstick. Rub with oil and sprinkle evenly with spice mixture.

2 Arrange drumsticks in air-fryer basket, spaced evenly apart, alternating ends. Place basket in air fryer and set temperature to 400 degrees. Cook until chicken is crisp and registers 195 degrees, 22 to 25 minutes, flipping and rotating chicken halfway through cooking. Transfer chicken to large plate, tent loosely with aluminum foil, and let rest for 5 minutes.

3 Meanwhile, microwave hot sauce, butter, molasses, and cornstarch in large bowl, stirring occasionally, until hot, about 1 minute. Add chicken and toss to coat. Transfer to serving platter and sprinkle with blue cheese. Serve.

TURKEY BURGERS

Serves 2

COOK TIME 12 minutes   **TOTAL TIME** 35 minutes

why this recipe works: The air fryer promises a convenient way to prepare turkey burgers for two, but it's not quite as simple as forming two ground-turkey patties and tossing them in the basket. On its own, ground turkey cooks up dry and dense—the extra-lean meat can't hold on to its own moisture during cooking. We found that mixing in a bit of Monterey Jack cheese went a long way in keeping the burgers moist, and the cheese crisped around the burger's edges, creating a crust. But to really keep the meat juicy, we added a mixture of sandwich bread and yogurt known as a panade. Acting like a sponge, this helped the burgers retain moisture and kept them from becoming too dense. Pressing a slight dimple in the raw patties prevented them from puffing up too much when they cooked. Be sure to use ground turkey, not ground turkey breast (also labeled 99 percent fat-free), or the burgers will be tough. You can use your air fryer to toast the buns; see page 13 for more information. Serve with your favorite burger toppings.

½ slice hearty white sandwich bread, crust removed, torn into ½-inch pieces

2 tablespoons plain yogurt

Salt and pepper

8 ounces ground turkey

1 ounce Monterey Jack cheese, shredded (¼ cup)

2 hamburger buns, toasted if desired

½ tomato, sliced thin

1 cup baby arugula

1 Mash bread, yogurt, ¼ teaspoon salt, and ¼ teaspoon pepper to paste in medium bowl using fork. Break up ground turkey into small pieces over bread mixture in bowl, add Monterey Jack, and lightly knead with hands until mixture forms cohesive mass.

2 Divide turkey mixture into 2 lightly packed balls, then gently flatten each into 1-inch-thick patty. Press center of each patty with your fingertips to create ¼-inch-deep depression. Season with salt and pepper.

3 Arrange patties in air-fryer basket, spaced evenly apart. Place basket in air fryer and set temperature to 350 degrees. Cook until burgers are browned and register 160 degrees, 12 to 16 minutes, flipping and rotating burgers halfway through cooking.

4 Transfer burgers to large plate, tent loosely with aluminum foil, and let rest for 5 minutes. Serve burgers on buns, topped with tomato and arugula.

TURKEY BURGERS WITH SUN-DRIED TOMATOES AND BASIL

Add ¼ cup sun-dried tomatoes, rinsed, patted dry, and chopped coarse, and 2 tablespoons chopped fresh basil to turkey mixture in step 1.

MINI GLAZED TURKEY MEATLOAVES

Serves 2

COOK TIME 25 minutes   **TOTAL TIME** 1 hour

why this recipe works It might come as a surprise that you can cook meatloaf in an air fryer, but we found that the circulated hot air was the ideal cooking environment for this comfort food classic. For a lighter version of meatloaf, we started with ground turkey, perking up its mild flavor with garlic, shallot, and thyme. Worcestershire sauce provided some savory meatiness, while cayenne added subtle heat. To hold the loaf together, we mixed in an egg and a panade made from white sandwich bread and milk, which also helped the meatloaf to remain moist. Shaping two free-form mini loaves, rather than one big loaf, enabled the dish to cook in just 25 minutes and provided more surface area to be glazed. We made a flavor-packed glaze from ketchup, cider vinegar, brown sugar, and hot sauce. To ensure that it stuck, we applied a first coat to the meatloaves and let them cook until the glaze was tacky, then added a second coat of glaze, which stuck to this base coat in an even layer. Since the loaves were delicate, we placed them on an aluminum foil sling, which allowed us to rotate and also remove them easily. Be sure to use ground turkey, not ground turkey breast (also labeled 99 percent fat-free). For more information on making a foil sling, see page 11.

1   shallot, minced

1   tablespoon
    vegetable oil

1   garlic clove, minced

½   teaspoon minced
    fresh thyme or
    ⅛ teaspoon dried

    Pinch cayenne pepper

1   slice hearty white
    sandwich bread,
    crust removed, torn
    into ½-inch pieces

1   large egg, lightly
    beaten

1   tablespoon whole
    milk

1   tablespoon
    Worcestershire sauce

¼   teaspoon salt

¼   teaspoon pepper

1   pound ground turkey

¼   cup ketchup

1   tablespoon cider
    vinegar

1   tablespoon packed
    brown sugar

½   teaspoon hot sauce

1 Make foil sling for air-fryer basket by folding 1 long sheet of aluminum foil so it is 4 inches wide. Lay sheet of foil widthwise across basket, pressing foil into and up sides of basket. Fold excess foil as needed so that edges of foil are flush with top of basket. Lightly spray foil and basket with vegetable oil spray.

2 Microwave shallot, oil, garlic, thyme, and cayenne in large bowl until fragrant, about 1 minute. Add bread, egg, milk, Worcestershire, salt, and pepper and mash mixture to paste using fork. Break up ground turkey into small pieces over bread mixture and knead with hands until well combined. Shape turkey mixture into two 5 by 3-inch loaves. Arrange loaves on sling in prepared basket, spaced evenly apart.

3 Combine ketchup, vinegar, sugar, and hot sauce in small bowl, then brush loaves with half of ketchup mixture. Place basket in air fryer and set temperature to 350 degrees. Cook until meatloaves register 160 degrees, 25 to 30 minutes, brushing with remaining ketchup mixture and rotating meatloaves using sling halfway through cooking.

4 Using foil sling, carefully remove meatloaves from basket. Tent loosely with foil and let rest for 5 minutes. Serve.

BEEF, PORK, AND LAMB

SPICE-RUBBED STEAK WITH SNAP PEA AND CUCUMBER SALAD

Serves 4

COOK TIME 15 minutes

TOTAL TIME 45 minutes

why this recipe works Looking to make juicy, perfectly cooked steak in the air fryer, we set our sights on 1½-inch-thick steak. These hefty cuts often command equally hefty prices, but we wanted a reasonably priced option ideal for an easy weeknight meal. Top sirloin, known for its lean texture and nice flavor, fit the bill. Cutting the steak into two pieces enabled it to fit snugly in the air fryer. Since the air fryer would essentially be roasting, rather than searing, the meat, we applied a fragrant spice rub to give it a bold crust. Rubbing the steak with a little oil first helped the spices adhere to the lean meat. We placed our steak in the air fryer and set it to 400 degrees to blast it with heat. Even with the circulated hot air, we found that flipping and rotating the pieces halfway through cooking produced more even results. After 15 minutes, our steaks emerged juicy and a perfect medium-rare. Since the beef could cook virtually unattended in the air fryer, we used the downtime to prepare a simple salad. Fresh snap peas, crisp radishes, and peppery baby arugula tossed in a creamy dill dressing offset the rich flavor of the spice-rubbed steak.

1½ teaspoons ground cumin

1½ teaspoons chili powder

Salt and pepper

¾ teaspoon ground coriander

⅛ teaspoon ground cinnamon

⅛ teaspoon cayenne pepper

1 (1½-pound) boneless top sirloin steak, 1½ inches thick, trimmed and halved crosswise

1 teaspoon plus 1½ tablespoons extra-virgin olive oil

3 tablespoons mayonnaise

1½ tablespoons white wine vinegar

1 tablespoon minced fresh dill

1 small garlic clove, minced

½ English cucumber, halved lengthwise and sliced thin

8 ounces sugar snap peas, strings removed, cut in half on bias

2 ounces (2 cups) baby arugula

2 radishes, trimmed, halved, and sliced thin

1 Combine cumin, chili powder, 1¼ teaspoons salt, ½ teaspoon pepper, coriander, cinnamon, and cayenne in bowl. Pat steaks dry with paper towels, rub with 1 teaspoon oil, and sprinkle evenly with spice mixture.

2 Arrange steaks in air-fryer basket, spaced evenly apart. Place basket in air fryer and set temperature to 400 degrees. Cook until steaks register 120 to 125 degrees (for medium-rare) or 130 to 135 degrees (for medium), 15 to 20 minutes, flipping and rotating steaks halfway through cooking. Transfer steaks to cutting board, tent with aluminum foil, and let rest while preparing salad.

3 Whisk remaining 1½ tablespoons oil, mayonnaise, vinegar, dill, garlic, ⅛ teaspoon salt, and ⅛ teaspoon pepper together in large bowl. Add cucumber, snap peas, arugula, and radishes and gently toss to combine. Season with salt and pepper to taste. Slice steaks and serve with salad.

TOP SIRLOIN STEAK WITH ROASTED MUSHROOMS AND BLUE CHEESE SAUCE

Serves 4

COOK TIME 25 minutes   **TOTAL TIME** 50 minutes

why this recipe works Steak with blue cheese sauce, golden-brown mushrooms, and tender onions is typically restaurant fare. For an unfussy version to make at home, we employed our air fryer to cook both steaks and vegetables in one go. We started with relatively inexpensive but well-marbled top sirloin and robust cremini mushrooms. Frozen pearl onions added a classy touch while keeping the prep light. Ensuring the steaks and vegetables finished cooking at the same time initially presented a challenge—they cooked at different rates and the mushrooms took up an awful lot of space in the basket. Our solution was to give the vegetables a head start. Since mushrooms shrink as they cook, we soon had room to rest our steaks on top; this arrangement also lifted our steaks closer to the air fryer's heating element, enhancing browning. While the steaks rested, we microwaved a little blue cheese and cream to create a simple sauce, then stirred in more blue cheese chunks for pleasant texture.

1½ pounds cremini mushrooms, trimmed and halved if large or left whole if small

1 cup frozen pearl onions, thawed

1 tablespoon extra-virgin olive oil

4 garlic cloves, minced

2 teaspoons minced fresh thyme or ½ teaspoon dried

Salt and pepper

1 (1½-pound) boneless top sirloin steak, 1½ inches thick, trimmed and halved crosswise

2 ounces blue cheese, crumbled (½ cup)

¼ cup heavy cream

1 tablespoon chopped fresh parsley

1 Toss mushrooms and onions with 2 teaspoons oil, garlic, thyme, and ½ teaspoon salt in bowl; transfer to air-fryer basket. Place basket in air fryer and set temperature to 400 degrees. Cook until mushrooms and onions begin to brown, 12 to 15 minutes, stirring halfway through cooking.

2 Pat steaks dry with paper towels, rub with remaining 1 teaspoon oil, and season with salt and pepper. Stir mushrooms and onions, then arrange steaks on top, spaced evenly apart. Return basket to air fryer and cook until steaks register 120 to 125 degrees (for medium-rare) or 130 to 135 degrees (for medium), 13 to 18 minutes, flipping and rotating steaks halfway through cooking. Transfer steaks to cutting board and mushroom-onion mixture to serving bowl. Tent each with aluminum foil and let rest while preparing sauce.

3 Microwave ¼ cup blue cheese and cream in bowl, whisking occasionally, until blue cheese is melted and smooth, about 30 seconds, stirring once halfway through. Let sauce cool slightly, then stir in remaining ¼ cup blue cheese. Stir parsley into mushroom-onion mixture and season with salt and pepper to taste. Slice steaks and serve with mushroom-onion mixture and sauce.

FLANK STEAK WITH ROASTED POTATOES AND CHIMICHURRI

Serves 2

COOK TIME 20 minutes

TOTAL TIME 45 minutes

why this recipe works Knowing the intense heat of the air fryer would do justice to both meat and potatoes, we set out to create a steakhouse-quality meal without dirtying a single pan. We started with lean, beefy flank steak, cutting it in half lengthwise to allow for better air-flow and more crust. Brushing the meat with honey as well as oil gave it a slightly better "sear" during its brief stint in the air fryer (the sugars in honey brown faster than proteins do). For our potatoes, extra-small Red Bliss potatoes were ideal as they could be simply tossed with olive oil, salt, and pepper and roasted whole. We gave the potatoes a 12-minute head start before stacking the steaks on top and letting both cook to perfection. While the meat rested, we whisked a quick chimichurri sauce from parsley, oregano, garlic, red pepper flakes, oil, and red wine vinegar. The grassy, herbaceous sauce tasted as good drizzled on the potatoes as it did on the meat. Use extra-small red potatoes measuring about 1 inch in diameter. If you can't find extra-small potatoes, substitute 1 pound of red potatoes cut into 1-inch pieces. Warming the honey makes it easier to brush onto the steaks.

- 1 pound extra-small Red Bliss potatoes, unpeeled
- 3 tablespoons extra-virgin olive oil
- Salt and pepper
- 2 teaspoons honey, warmed
- 1 (12-ounce) flank steak, trimmed and halved with grain
- 2 tablespoons minced fresh parsley
- 1½ teaspoons red wine vinegar
- 1½ teaspoons minced fresh oregano or ½ teaspoon dried
- 1 garlic clove, minced
- ⅛ teaspoon red pepper flakes

1 Toss red potatoes with 2 teaspoons oil, ¼ teaspoon salt, and ¼ teaspoon pepper in bowl; transfer to air-fryer basket. Place basket in air fryer, set temperature to 400 degrees, and cook for 12 minutes.

2 Combine honey and 1 teaspoon oil in small bowl. Pat steaks dry with paper towels, brush with honey-oil mixture, and season with salt and pepper. Arrange steaks on top of potatoes, spaced evenly apart. Return basket to air fryer and cook until steaks are browned and register 120 to 125 degrees (for medium-rare) or 130 to 135 degrees (for medium), 8 to 10 minutes, flipping and rotating steaks halfway through cooking. Transfer steaks to cutting board and potatoes to serving bowl. Tent each with aluminum foil and let rest while preparing chimichurri.

3 Combine remaining 2 tablespoons oil, parsley, vinegar, oregano, garlic, and pepper flakes in separate bowl and season with salt and pepper to taste. Slice steaks thin against grain and serve with potatoes and chimichurri.

KOREAN STEAK TIPS WITH NAPA CABBAGE SLAW

Serves 4

COOK TIME 13 minutes   **TOTAL TIME** 45 minutes

why this recipe works Inspired by Korean barbecue, these succulent morsels of beef offer a fantastic combination of spicy, sweet, sour, and salty flavors. We built a simple but authentic marinade by blooming ginger and garlic with sesame oil in the microwave, then whisking in honey, *gochujang* (a Korean chili paste), and soy sauce. We used this to coat sirloin steak tips; the combo was so tender and flavorful, the meat needed no marinating period but could be cooked straightaway in the air fryer. For contrast, we made a crunchy napa cabbage and carrot slaw, tossing it in a bright but not overly sharp rice vinegar dressing. Sprinkling the beef with scallions and sesame seeds added a fresh and toasty finish. Sirloin steak tips, also called flap meat, are sold as whole steaks, cubes, and strips. To ensure uniform pieces, we prefer to purchase whole steak tips and cut them ourselves. Gochujang can be found in Asian markets and some supermarkets. If you can't find it, substitute an equal amount of sriracha.

- 2 tablespoons toasted sesame oil
- 2 teaspoons grated fresh ginger
- 1 garlic clove, minced to paste
- 2 tablespoons honey
- 2 tablespoons gochujang

- 1 teaspoon plus 1 tablespoon soy sauce
- 1½ pounds sirloin steak tips, trimmed and cut into 2-inch pieces
- 3 tablespoons rice vinegar

- ½ small head napa cabbage, cored and sliced thin (4 cups)
- 1 carrot, peeled and grated
- 2 tablespoons toasted sesame seeds
- 3 scallions, sliced thin on bias

1 Microwave 1 tablespoon oil, 1 teaspoon ginger, and garlic in large bowl until fragrant, about 30 seconds, stirring once halfway through. Whisk in 4 teaspoons honey, gochujang, and 1 teaspoon soy sauce until smooth. Add steak tips and toss to coat.

2 Arrange steak tips in air-fryer basket, spaced evenly apart. Place basket in air fryer and set temperature to 400 degrees. Cook until steak tips are lightly browned and register 130 to 135 degrees (for medium), 13 to 18 minutes, flipping and rotating steak tips halfway through cooking. Transfer steak tips to serving platter, tent with aluminum foil, and let rest while preparing slaw.

3 Whisk vinegar, remaining 1 tablespoon oil, remaining 1 teaspoon ginger, remaining 2 teaspoons honey, and remaining 1 tablespoon soy sauce together in large bowl. Add cabbage and carrot and toss to coat. Let sit for 5 minutes, then stir in 1 tablespoon sesame seeds. Sprinkle steak tips with remaining 1 tablespoon sesame seeds and scallions and serve with slaw.

COFFEE- AND FENNEL-RUBBED BONELESS SHORT RIBS WITH CELERY ROOT SALAD

Serves 2

COOK TIME 38 minutes   **TOTAL TIME** 1 hour

why this recipe works We associate short ribs with slow braising, but boneless short ribs (which are cut from a less tough part of the cow than bone-in short ribs) can be roasted with excellent results, yielding tender meat with deep savor. Two slabs fit neatly in the air fryer, offering a hands-off, luxurious meal for two. For a seasoning that stood up to the rich meat, we applied a fennel-coffee rub. Since there was room in the basket, we added a vegetable; subtly sweet celery root was a perfect pairing. We roasted the celery root at 400 degrees until it just became tender, then added our short ribs and lowered the temperature to 250 degrees to let the meat cook gently and evenly. A sprinkle of pomegranate seeds and parsley brightened the earthy celery root. The thickness and marbling of boneless short ribs can vary; look for lean ribs cut from the chuck. Do not substitute bone-in English-style short ribs. Because they are cooked gently and not seared, the short ribs will be rosy throughout.

- 2 pounds celery root, peeled and cut into ¾-inch pieces
- 2 tablespoons extra-virgin olive oil
- Salt and pepper
- 1½ teaspoons ground fennel

- 1 teaspoon ground coffee
- 1 teaspoon packed brown sugar
- ½ teaspoon garlic powder

- 12 ounces boneless short ribs, 1½ to 2 inches thick and 4 to 5 inches long, trimmed
- ½ cup pomegranate seeds
- ½ cup fresh parsley leaves
- 1 teaspoon lemon juice

1 Toss celery root with 2 teaspoons oil, ⅛ teaspoon salt, and ⅛ teaspoon pepper in bowl; transfer to air-fryer basket. Place basket in air fryer and set temperature to 400 degrees. Cook celery root until just tender, about 20 minutes, tossing halfway through cooking.

2 Combine fennel, coffee, sugar, garlic powder, ¼ teaspoon salt, and ¼ teaspoon pepper in small bowl. Pat short ribs dry with paper towels, rub with 1 teaspoon oil, and sprinkle evenly with spice mixture.

3 Stir celery root, then arrange short ribs on top, spaced evenly apart. Return basket to air fryer and set temperature to 250 degrees. Cook until beef registers 130 to 135 degrees (for medium) and celery root is tender, 18 to 24 minutes, flipping and rotating short ribs halfway through cooking. Transfer short ribs to cutting board, tent with aluminum foil, and let rest while preparing salad.

4 Transfer celery root to large bowl, add pomegranate seeds, parsley, lemon juice, and remaining 1 tablespoon oil, and toss to coat. Slice short ribs thin and serve with salad.

ROASTED BONELESS SHORT RIBS WITH RED PEPPER RELISH

Serves 4

COOK TIME 18 minutes   **TOTAL TIME** 35 minutes

why this recipe works In Argentina, short ribs are often cooked over hardwood coals until tender, smoky, and rosy within. To replicate this in our air fryer, we started with boneless short ribs, "slow-roasting" them at 250 degrees until evenly cooked (in reality, this took only 18 minutes). As they roasted, the wire basket allowed excess fat to drip away. A spice rub of smoked paprika, brown sugar, and cumin gave our ribs a smoky flavor reminiscent of grilling. To cut the richness, we prepared a piquant red pepper relish. To avoid using the stovetop, we microwaved red bell pepper with minced shallot, olive oil, garlic, and a pinch of cayenne until the bell pepper was softened. Cilantro and lemon juice brought freshness and balanced the acidity. The thickness and marbling of boneless short ribs can vary; look for lean ribs cut from the chuck. Do not substitute bone-in English-style short ribs. Because they are cooked gently and not seared, the short ribs will be rosy throughout.

- 2 teaspoons smoked paprika
- 2 teaspoons packed brown sugar
- 1½ teaspoons ground cumin
- Salt and pepper

- 1½ pounds boneless short ribs, 1½ to 2 inches thick and 4 to 5 inches long, trimmed
- 2 teaspoons plus 2 tablespoons extra-virgin olive oil
- ¼ cup finely chopped red bell pepper

- 1 small shallot, minced
- 2 garlic cloves, minced
- Pinch cayenne pepper
- 2 tablespoons minced fresh cilantro
- 2 teaspoons lemon juice

1 Combine paprika, sugar, cumin, ½ teaspoon salt, and ¼ teaspoon pepper in bowl. Pat short ribs dry with paper towels, rub with 2 teaspoons oil, and sprinkle evenly with spice mixture. Arrange short ribs in air-fryer basket, spaced evenly apart. Place basket in air fryer and set temperature to 250 degrees. Cook until beef registers 130 to 135 degrees (for medium), 18 to 24 minutes, flipping and rotating short ribs halfway through cooking. Transfer short ribs to cutting board, tent with aluminum foil, and let rest while preparing relish.

2 Microwave bell pepper, shallot, garlic, cayenne, ⅛ teaspoon salt, and remaining 2 tablespoons oil in bowl, stirring occasionally, until vegetables are softened, about 2 minutes. Let cool slightly, then stir in cilantro and lemon juice. Season with salt and pepper to taste. Slice short ribs thin and serve with relish.

GINGER-SOY BEEF AND VEGETABLE KEBABS

Serves 2

COOK TIME 18 minutes   **TOTAL TIME** 1 hour

why this recipe works Whether you cook beef and vegetable kebabs on the grill or in the air fryer, the advice is the same: Resist the urge to thread both meat and veggies onto a single skewer! This arrangement may look pretty, but the meat will likely dry out long before the vegetables are done. For juicy chunks of beef and browned, tender-firm vegetables, we first chose well-marbled steak tips, cutting them into generous 1½-inch cubes. A quick ginger-soy marinade added deep flavor in 10 minutes, and we reserved some for a sauce. Meanwhile, we cooked our vegetable skewers—a mix of red onion, shiitake mushrooms, and zucchini. Partway through cooking, we stacked our beef kebabs on top, placed crosswise for maximum air circulation; this also brought the meat closer to the heat source for better browning. Soon our kebabs all emerged perfectly cooked. Sirloin steak tips, also called flap meat, are sold as whole steaks, cubes, and strips. To ensure uniform pieces, we prefer to purchase whole steak tips and cut them ourselves.

2 tablespoons vegetable oil	1½ teaspoons honey	4 ounces shiitake mushrooms, stemmed and halved if large
1 teaspoon grated fresh ginger	½ teaspoon grated orange zest plus 1 tablespoon juice	
1 garlic clove, minced	12 ounces sirloin steak tips, trimmed and cut into 1½-inch pieces	1 zucchini, sliced into ½-inch-thick rounds
¼ teaspoon red pepper flakes		¼ teaspoon salt
1 tablespoon toasted sesame oil	1 small red onion, halved and cut through root end into 6 equal wedges	¼ teaspoon pepper
2 teaspoons soy sauce		5 (6-inch) wooden skewers

1 Microwave 4 teaspoons vegetable oil, ginger, garlic, and pepper flakes in large bowl until fragrant, about 30 seconds, stirring once halfway through. Whisk in sesame oil, soy sauce, honey, and orange zest and juice until combined. Measure out and reserve 3 tablespoons oil mixture. Add beef to remaining oil mixture and toss to coat; set aside.

2 Meanwhile, toss red onion, mushrooms, and zucchini with remaining 2 teaspoons vegetable oil, salt, and pepper in bowl. Thread 1 piece of onion onto wooden skewer. Thread one-third of zucchini and mushrooms onto skewer, followed by second piece of onion. Repeat skewering remaining vegetables with 2 more skewers. Arrange skewers in air-fryer basket, parallel to each other and spaced evenly apart. Place basket in air fryer and set temperature to 400 degrees. Cook until vegetables are beginning to brown, about 8 minutes.

3 While vegetable skewers cook, thread beef evenly onto remaining 2 skewers. Flip and rotate vegetable skewers, then arrange beef skewers on top, perpendicular to vegetable skewers. Return basket to air fryer and cook until beef registers 130 to 135 degrees (for medium) and vegetables are crisp-tender, 10 to 14 minutes, flipping and rotating beef skewers halfway through cooking.

4 Transfer skewers to serving platter, tent with aluminum foil, and let rest for 5 minutes. Whisk reserved oil mixture to recombine. Using fork, push beef and vegetables off skewers onto platter and drizzle with oil mixture. Serve.

BEEF SATAY WITH RED CURRY NOODLES

Serves 2

COOK TIME 6 minutes   **TOTAL TIME** 1 hour

why this recipe works Topped with "air-grilled" skewers of seasoned beef, this red curry noodle bowl is like two meals in one yet requires far less juggling than such dishes typically do. Air-frying the beef, rather than grilling it, vastly streamlined the process and let us focus on the noodles. We coated sliced flank steak with a brown sugar–coriander mixture that would complement our red curry sauce, then threaded the slices onto skewers, which we stacked in the air fryer in a crisscross pattern for optimal air circulation. To build an easy noodle bowl, we used thin vermicelli noodles, which needed only a quick soak in boiling water. Strips of bell pepper and snow peas required no cooking and added color and crunch. To create an easy sauce with multidimensional flavor, we microwaved coconut milk and red curry paste to bloom the flavors. Adding lime juice, sugar, and fish sauce gave us a sauce that incorporated each taste: salty, sweet, sour, bitter, and umami. A final sprinkling of chopped basil added pleasant freshness to complete our noodle bowl.

1 tablespoon packed light brown sugar	10 (6-inch) wooden skewers	1 small red bell pepper, stemmed, seeded, and cut into 2-inch-long matchsticks
2 teaspoons vegetable oil	4 ounces rice vermicelli	
1 teaspoon ground coriander	½ cup canned coconut milk	4 ounces snow peas, strings removed and sliced lengthwise into matchsticks
¼ teaspoon salt	2 teaspoons Thai red curry paste	
⅛ teaspoon cayenne pepper	1 tablespoon lime juice, plus extra for seasoning	½ cup chopped fresh basil
1 (12-ounce) flank steak, ½ to ¾ inch thick, trimmed	2 teaspoons fish sauce, plus extra for seasoning	

1 Combine 1 teaspoon sugar, oil, coriander, salt, and cayenne in bowl. Slice steak against grain into ½-inch-thick slices (you should have at least 10 slices) and pat dry with paper towels. Add beef to sugar mixture and toss to coat. Weave beef evenly onto skewers, leaving 1 inch at bottom of skewer exposed.

2 Arrange half of beef skewers in air-fryer basket, parallel to each other and spaced evenly apart. Arrange remaining skewers on top, perpendicular to bottom layer. Place basket in air fryer and set temperature to 400 degrees. Cook until beef is lightly browned, 6 to 8 minutes, flipping and rotating skewers twice during cooking. Transfer skewers to serving platter, tent with aluminum foil, and let rest while preparing noodles.

3 Place noodles in large bowl and pour 6 cups boiling water over top. Stir noodles briefly to ensure they are completely submerged, then let soak, stirring occasionally, until tender, about 2 minutes. Drain noodles and set aside.

4 Whisk coconut milk, red curry paste, and remaining 2 teaspoons sugar together in now-empty bowl and microwave until fragrant, about 1 minute. Whisk in lime juice and fish sauce. Add noodles, bell pepper, snow peas, and basil and gently toss to coat. Season with extra lime juice and fish sauce to taste. Adjust consistency with hot water as needed. Serve beef skewers with noodles.

BIG ITALIAN MEATBALLS WITH ZUCCHINI NOODLES

Serves 2

COOK TIME 35 minutes   **TOTAL TIME** 1 hour

why this recipe works Unexpected but wonderful, this air-fryer take on spaghetti and meatballs offers a lightened-up and utterly simple way to enjoy the comfort classic. How do you air-fry spaghetti? Trade starchy pasta for spiralized zucchini, which cooks in minutes in the air fryer, eliminating the need to boil a pot of water. To top our noodles, four giant meatballs seemed more fun than smaller ones. A milk and bread panade kept the meatballs tender and moist (it also held them together). Parmesan cheese, basil, a shallot, garlic powder, and an egg gave them richness and flavor. We cooked the oversize meatballs at a low temperature to prevent the exterior from drying out before the middle was done. Spiralized zucchini noodles can be found in the produce section of the supermarket. If you own a spiralizer, two 12-ounce zucchini will yield the necessary amount of zucchini noodles for this recipe.

- 1 slice hearty white sandwich bread, crust removed, torn into ½-inch pieces
- 1 large egg
- 3 tablespoons milk
- 1 shallot, minced
- 1 ounce Parmesan cheese, grated (½ cup), plus extra for serving
- ¼ cup chopped fresh basil
- 1 teaspoon garlic powder
- Salt and pepper
- 1 pound 93 percent lean ground beef
- 1 pound zucchini noodles
- 2 teaspoons extra-virgin olive oil
- ¾ cup jarred marinara sauce, warmed

1 Mash bread, egg, and milk into paste in large bowl using fork. Stir in shallot, Parmesan, 2 tablespoons basil, garlic powder, ¼ teaspoon salt, and ¼ teaspoon pepper. Break up ground beef into small pieces over bread mixture in bowl and lightly knead with hands until well combined. Pinch off and roll mixture into four meatballs.

2 Arrange meatballs in air-fryer basket, spaced evenly apart. Place basket in air fryer, set temperature to 250 degrees, and cook for 20 minutes. Flip and rotate meatballs and continue to cook until well browned and register 160 degrees, 10 to 15 minutes. Transfer meatballs to serving platter, tent with aluminum foil, and let rest while preparing noodles.

3 Toss zucchini noodles in clean bowl with oil and season with salt and pepper. Arrange noodles in even layer in now-empty air-fryer basket. Return basket to air fryer and set temperature to 400 degrees. Cook until noodles are just tender, 5 to 7 minutes. Divide zucchini noodles and meatballs between individual serving bowls and top with warm marinara sauce. Sprinkle with remaining 2 tablespoons basil and serve, passing extra Parmesan separately.

JUICY WELL-DONE CHEESEBURGERS

Serves 2

COOK TIME 19 minutes　　　　　　　　　**TOTAL TIME** 30 minutes

why this recipe works Typical burger recipes require hovering over a hot pan or grill, waiting for the right moment to flip the patties to avoid turning out a dry hockey puck. But not this one—and not only because the air fryer's timer tells you when they need flipping. The real key was using a panade of mashed bread and milk, which kept the patties moist and juicy even when cooked to well-done. How? The bread's starches swell when mixed with liquid, forming a gel that holds juices in and prevents meat proteins from toughening when cooked. Giving the burgers a slight dimple in the middle before cooking also prevented them from puffing up in the hot air. With our burgers done, we wondered if we could use the air fryer to cook other burger components, and found it could toast hamburger buns (see page 13) and even caramelize onions for our onion and blue cheese variation. Serve with your favorite burger toppings.

½ slice hearty white sandwich bread, crust removed, torn into ¼-inch pieces

1 tablespoon milk

½ teaspoon garlic powder

½ teaspoon onion powder

12 ounces 85 percent lean ground beef

Salt and pepper

2 slices American cheese (2 ounces)

2 hamburger buns, toasted if desired

1 Mash bread, milk, garlic powder, and onion powder into paste in medium bowl using fork. Break up ground beef into small pieces over bread mixture in bowl and lightly knead with hands until well combined. Divide mixture into 2 lightly packed balls, then gently flatten each into 1-inch-thick patty. Press center of each patty with fingertips to create ¼-inch-deep depression. Season with salt and pepper.

2 Arrange patties in air-fryer basket, spaced evenly apart. Place basket in air fryer and set temperature to 350 degrees. Cook until burgers are lightly browned and register 140 to 145 degrees (for medium-well) or 150 to 155 degrees (for well-done), 18 to 21 minutes, flipping and rotating burgers halfway through cooking.

3 Top each burger with 1 slice cheese. Return basket to air fryer and cook until cheese is melted, about 30 seconds. Serve burgers on buns.

JUICY WELL-DONE GREEN CHILE CHEESEBURGERS

Omit onion powder. Substitute pepper Jack cheese for American cheese. Add ¼ cup canned chopped green chiles, drained and patted dry, to beef mixture in step 1.

JUICY WELL-DONE BURGERS WITH CARAMELIZED ONIONS AND BLUE CHEESE

Omit onion powder. Substitute ¼ cup crumbled blue cheese for American cheese. Slice 1 small red onion into ¼-inch-thick rounds, then separate rounds into rings. Toss onion rings with 1 teaspoon vegetable oil, ¼ teaspoon sugar, and ⅛ teaspoon salt in bowl. Arrange onion rings evenly in air-fryer basket, then place patties on top and cook as directed in step 2. Top burgers with caramelized onions before serving.

STEAK TACOS

Serves 2 to 4

COOK TIME 13 minutes **TOTAL TIME** 40 minutes

why this recipe works When a taco craving strikes, the air fryer is a cook's best friend. With little oversight—thanks to its regulated heat and built-in timer—this automated sous chef turned out juicy, perfectly cooked steak (flank steak offered nice beefy flavor; cutting it in half sped up the cooking) while we warmed tortillas and prepared a few garnishes. For a hands-off, zingy topping, we quick-pickled sliced red onion, jalapeño, and radishes, letting the vegetables steep until crisp-tender in a hot mixture of red wine vinegar and sugar while the steak cooked. To finish, crumbled *queso fresco* and sliced avocado added pleasant richness, and cilantro leaves gave our tacos a pop of freshness.

- 1 cup red wine vinegar
- ⅓ cup sugar
- ½ red onion, sliced thin
- 2 radishes, trimmed, halved, and sliced thin
- 1 jalapeño chile, stemmed and sliced thin into rounds

- 1 (1-pound) flank steak, trimmed and halved with grain
- 1 teaspoon vegetable oil
- ¾ teaspoon ground cumin
- Salt and pepper
- 6–12 (6-inch) corn tortillas, warmed

- 2 ounces queso fresco, crumbled (½ cup)
- 1 avocado, halved, pitted, and sliced thin
- Fresh cilantro leaves
- Lime wedges

1 Microwave vinegar and sugar in medium bowl until steaming, about 5 minutes. Stir in onion, radishes, and jalapeño and set aside.

2 Pat steaks dry with paper towels. Rub steaks with oil, sprinkle with cumin, and season with salt and pepper. Arrange steaks in air-fryer basket, spaced evenly apart. Place basket in air fryer and set temperature to 400 degrees. Cook until steaks are browned and register 120 to 125 degrees (for medium-rare) or 130 to 135 degrees (for medium), 13 to 18 minutes, flipping and rotating steaks halfway through cooking. Transfer steaks to cutting board, tent with aluminum foil, and let rest for 5 minutes.

3 Drain pickled vegetables and return to now-empty bowl. Slice steaks thin against grain. Serve with warm tortillas, pickled vegetables, queso fresco, avocado, cilantro, and lime wedges.

SOUTHWESTERN BEEF HAND PIES

Makes 8 pies

COOK TIME 12 minutes   **TOTAL TIME** 1 hour, plus freezing time

why this recipe works Easily prepared with store-bought pie dough, these spiced ground-beef hand pies can be made ahead and frozen, then quickly baked in the air fryer for a flaky, steaming-hot snack or meal anytime. Microwaving beef, aromatics, and spices bloomed flavors and let us drain away excess liquid that would sog out the dough. We then stirred in cheese, which added richness and created a cohesive filling; salsa for depth of flavor; and cilantro for freshness. We were able to cut eight 5-inch rounds from two 12-inch pastry rounds to make four hand pies. Hand pies can also be cooked immediately without freezing; reduce the cooking time in step 3 to 10 to 12 minutes.

- 8 ounces 93 percent lean ground beef
- 3 garlic cloves, minced
- 2 teaspoons chili powder
- 1 teaspoon ground cumin
- 1 teaspoon minced fresh oregano or ¼ teaspoon dried
- 4 ounces Monterey Jack cheese, shredded (1 cup)
- 1 cup mild tomato salsa, drained
- 2 tablespoons chopped fresh cilantro
- 1 package store-bought pie dough
- 1 large egg, lightly beaten

1 Microwave beef, garlic, chili powder, cumin, and oregano in bowl, stirring occasionally and breaking up meat with wooden spoon, until beef is no longer pink, about 3 minutes. Transfer beef mixture to fine-mesh strainer set over large bowl and let drain for 10 minutes; discard juices. Return drained beef mixture to now-empty bowl and stir in Monterey Jack, salsa, and cilantro.

2 Roll 1 dough round into 12-inch circle on lightly floured counter. Using 5-inch round biscuit cutter, stamp out 4 rounds; discard dough scraps. Repeat with remaining dough round. Mound beef mixture evenly in center of each stamped round. Fold dough over filling and crimp edges with fork to seal. Transfer hand pies to parchment paper–lined rimmed baking sheet, brush with egg, and freeze until firm, about 1 hour. (Hand pies can be transferred to zipper-lock bag and stored in freezer for up to 2 weeks; do not thaw before cooking.)

3 to cook hand pies Lightly spray base of air-fryer basket with vegetable oil spray. Arrange up to 2 hand pies in prepared basket, spaced evenly apart. Place basket in air fryer and set temperature to 350 degrees. Cook until hand pies are golden brown, 12 to 15 minutes. Transfer to wire rack and let cool slightly. Serve.

SOUTHWESTERN BEAN AND CORN HAND PIES

Omit ground beef. Substitute 1 cup drained tomatillo salsa (salsa verde) for tomato salsa. Add 1 tablespoon extra-virgin olive oil to spice mixture in step 1 and microwave until fragrant, about 30 seconds. Stir 1¼ cups canned black beans, rinsed, and ¾ cup frozen corn into spice mixture with Monterey Jack.

CRISPY BREADED BONELESS PORK CHOPS

Serves 2

COOK TIME 18 minutes   **TOTAL TIME** 45 minutes

why this recipe works We wanted juicy, perfectly cooked pork chops wrapped in a crispy and deeply flavored crust. But since air fryers don't fry in the same way that a hot pan with oil does, we had trouble achieving a well-browned, crisp crust. Pretoasting the breading in the microwave with a little melted butter helped significantly, but it was when we switched from regular bread crumbs to Japanese panko that we achieved a crust with crunch. As with our chicken cutlets, we streamlined the dredging process by whisking the egg and flour together, but went a step further, packing a ton of flavor into the egg mixture with a double dose of mustard—Dijon and dry mustard—as well as garlic powder and cayenne pepper. However, the crumb topping flaked off when we flipped the chops during cooking. To help it stick, we scored the surface of the chops in a crosshatch pattern, creating additional surface area for the coating to cling to. We also cut two slits into the fat on the edges of the chops to prevent them from buckling in the hot air. Air frying for 18 minutes gave us the juicy chops we were after, and a squeeze from a lemon wedge added pleasant brightness.

¾ cup panko bread crumbs	1 tablespoon all-purpose flour	¼ teaspoon cayenne pepper
2 tablespoons unsalted butter, melted	1½ teaspoons dry mustard	2 (8-ounce) boneless pork chops, 1½ inches thick, trimmed
1 large egg	½ teaspoon garlic powder	
2 tablespoons Dijon mustard	¼ teaspoon salt	Lemon wedges

1 Toss panko with melted butter in bowl until evenly coated. Microwave, stirring frequently, until light golden brown, 1 to 3 minutes; transfer to shallow dish. Whisk egg, Dijon mustard, flour, dry mustard, garlic powder, salt, and cayenne together in second shallow dish.

2 Pat chops dry with paper towels. Using sharp knife, cut 2 slits, about 2 inches apart, through fat on edges of each chop. Cut ¹⁄₁₆-inch-deep slits, spaced ½ inch apart, in crosshatch pattern on both sides of chops. Working with 1 chop at a time, dredge in egg mixture, letting excess drip off, then coat with panko mixture, pressing gently to adhere.

3 Lightly spray base of air-fryer basket with vegetable oil spray. Arrange chops in prepared basket, spaced evenly apart. Place basket in air fryer and set temperature to 400 degrees. Cook until pork registers 140 degrees, 18 to 22 minutes, flipping and rotating chops halfway through cooking. Serve with lemon wedges.

ROASTED BONE-IN PORK CHOP

Serves 2

COOK TIME 20 minutes   **TOTAL TIME** 40 minutes

why this recipe works A bone-in pork chop offers a simple but special meal, with meat that's juicy and full of flavor down to the last gnaw of the bone. Aiming to roast bone-in pork chops for two in our air fryer, we first tried using two 8-ounce chops, but rotating and flipping them proved too awkward; they didn't quite fit. Since bone-in chops are often found thick-cut, we switched to a single 1-pound chop, which was sufficient for two people and easier to fit in the basket, and it made for a dramatic presentation. With such a thick chop, however, we needed a way to cook the meat through without the exterior drying out. While 400 degrees promised better browning, the intense heat dried out the sizable cut too quickly. Roasting at a more moderate 350 degrees resulted in an evenly cooked, juicy chop, and—to our pleasant surprise— also gave the chop more color because of the longer roasting time. Cutting two slits in the sides of the chop prevented it from curling during cooking. To contrast with the rich, roasted meat, we created two bold sauces, a peach-mustard sauce (made with frozen peaches) and an herbaceous, smoky chermoula. If making the chermoula, prepare it before roasting the chops to allow its flavors to meld.

1 (1-pound) bone-in pork rib or center-cut chop, 1½ to 1¾ inches thick, trimmed

1 teaspoon vegetable oil

Salt and pepper

1 Pat chop dry with paper towels. Using sharp knife, cut 2 slits, about 2 inches apart, through fat on edge of chop. Rub with oil and season with salt and pepper.

2 Place chop in air-fryer basket, then place basket in air fryer. Set temperature to 350 degrees and cook until pork registers 140 degrees, 20 to 25 minutes, flipping and rotating chop halfway through cooking.

3 Transfer chop to cutting board, tent with aluminum foil, and let rest for 5 minutes. Carve pork from bone and slice ½ inch thick. Serve.

PEACH-MUSTARD SAUCE
Microwave 5 ounces frozen sliced peaches, cut into 1-inch pieces, 2 tablespoons water, 1 tablespoon sugar, and 2 teaspoons white wine vinegar in medium bowl, stirring occasionally, until peaches have softened and mixture is slightly thickened, about 8 minutes. Let cool slightly, then stir in ¾ teaspoon whole-grain mustard and ½ teaspoon minced fresh thyme or rosemary.

CHERMOULA
Whisk ⅓ cup extra-virgin olive oil, ⅓ cup minced fresh cilantro, 1 tablespoon lemon juice, 2 minced garlic cloves, ½ teaspoon ground cumin, ½ teaspoon paprika, and ⅛ teaspoon cayenne in bowl until combined. Season with salt and pepper to taste.

LEMON-OREGANO ROASTED PORK CHOPS WITH TOMATO-FETA SALAD

Serves 2

COOK TIME 16 minutes   **TOTAL TIME** 50 minutes

why this recipe works Boneless pork chops make an easy weeknight meal and become especially convenient when cooked in an air fryer as opposed to grilling or pan frying. Because the boneless meat can dry out quickly, we set the maximum heat of 400 degrees, which ensured the chops stayed moist and juicy, but they needed a boost of color, particularly at the center, which didn't get as brown as the fattier edges. To boost browning, we tried elevating the chops closer to the heating element by placing them on a ring made of aluminum foil, but turning the chops was awkward and our makeshift ring stuck to the meat. Knowing that browning happens when sugars and proteins react with heat, we next brushed the chops lightly with honey, which is especially good for browning because of its high fructose content, giving our chops more color. We added flavor by mixing the honey with fresh oregano, garlic, and lemon zest. A zingy salad of cherry tomatoes, arugula, and feta came together while the meat rested. We tossed it with a creamy, lemon-yogurt dressing, adding in more oregano to echo the chops' flavor.

- 2 tablespoons minced fresh oregano
- 2 teaspoons plus 2 tablespoons extra-virgin olive oil
- 2 teaspoons honey
- 2 garlic cloves, minced

- 1½ teaspoons grated lemon zest plus 2 teaspoons juice
- 2 (8-ounce) boneless pork chops, about 1½ inches thick, trimmed
- Salt and pepper

- 2 tablespoons plain yogurt
- 12 ounces cherry tomatoes, halved
- 1 cup baby arugula
- 2 ounces feta cheese, crumbled (½ cup)
- 1 small shallot, sliced thin

1 Microwave 1 tablespoon oregano, 2 teaspoons oil, honey, half of garlic, and ½ teaspoon lemon zest in bowl until fragrant, about 30 seconds, stirring once halfway through.

2 Pat chops dry with paper towels. Using sharp knife, cut 2 slits, about 2 inches apart, through fat on edges of each chop. Brush chops with oil mixture and season with salt and pepper. Arrange chops in air-fryer basket, spaced evenly apart. Place basket in air fryer and set temperature to 400 degrees. Cook until pork registers 140 degrees,

16 to 20 minutes, flipping and rotating chops halfway through cooking. Transfer chops to plate, tent with aluminum foil, and let rest while making salad.

3 Whisk yogurt, remaining 2 tablespoons oil, remaining 1 tablespoon oregano, remaining garlic, remaining 1 teaspoon lemon zest, lemon juice, ¼ teaspoon salt, and ¼ teaspoon pepper together in large bowl. Add tomatoes, arugula, feta, and shallot and toss to coat. Season with salt and pepper to taste. Serve chops with salad.

FENNEL-RUBBED PORK TENDERLOIN WITH ZUCCHINI RIBBON SALAD

Serves 4

COOK TIME 16 minutes   **TOTAL TIME** 50 minutes

why this recipe works Mild, buttery pork tenderloin is a favorite choice for a weeknight meal, but its long shape wasn't an obvious fit for the air fryer. The solution? We cut it in half and found we could accommodate two tenderloins in the basket that way. Since the pork benefits from a crust, we brushed on a mixture of garlic, honey, lemon zest, and fennel seeds. Coarsely ground whole fennel seeds gave the meat a beautiful flavor and aroma. For an easy side dish, we shaved ribbons of zucchini, showcasing the squash's crunchier side. We tossed it with toasted pine nuts, basil, and shaved Parmesan, dressing the salad just before serving to avoid wilting. Use a spice grinder to coarsely grind the fennel (about six 1-second pulses); you can also pound the seeds with a skillet or meat mallet. Use a vegetable peeler or a mandoline to shave the zucchini. You can toast pine nuts in your air fryer; see page 13.

- ¼ cup extra-virgin olive oil
- 4 garlic cloves, minced
- 1 tablespoon honey
- 1 teaspoon grated lemon zest plus 2 tablespoons juice
- Salt and pepper

- 2 (1-pound) pork tenderloins, trimmed and halved crosswise
- 2 tablespoons fennel seeds, coarsely ground
- 4 small zucchini (6 ounces each), shaved lengthwise into ribbons

- 2 ounces Parmesan cheese, shaved
- 2 tablespoons shredded fresh basil
- 2 tablespoons pine nuts, toasted (optional)

1 Microwave 1 tablespoon oil, garlic, honey, lemon zest, ½ teaspoon salt, and ¼ teaspoon pepper in large bowl until fragrant, about 30 seconds, stirring once halfway through. Pat pork dry with paper towels, add to oil mixture, and toss to coat.

2 Sprinkle pork pieces with fennel seeds, pressing to adhere, then arrange in air fryer basket. (Tuck thinner tail ends of tenderloins under themselves as needed to create uniform pieces.) Place basket in air fryer and set temperature to 350 degrees. Cook until pork is lightly browned and registers 140 degrees, 16 to 21 minutes, flipping and rotating tenderloin pieces halfway through cooking. Transfer pork to cutting board, tent with aluminum foil, and let rest while preparing salad.

3 Gently toss zucchini with remaining 3 tablespoons oil, lemon juice, ¼ teaspoon salt, and ¼ teaspoon pepper in clean bowl. Arrange attractively on serving platter and sprinkle with Parmesan, basil, and pine nuts, if using. Slice pork ½ inch thick and serve with salad.

PORK TENDERLOIN WITH PROSCIUTTO AND SAGE

Serves 4

COOK TIME 20 minutes   **TOTAL TIME** 45 minutes

why this recipe works Inspired by saltimbocca, the Roman dish of veal cutlets topped with prosciutto and sage, these savory bundles deliver a fancy meal with absurdly little effort. We started with pork tenderloin, which, like veal, is mild and tender but is easier to find and pairs beautifully with sage. While getting prosciutto to adhere to veal cutlets can be a fussy business involving toothpicks, here we simply halved two pork tenderloins to create four portions and wrapped each in prosciutto—layering fresh sage leaves in between—to create an attractive parcel, brushing melted butter both under and over the prosciutto; this step helped it to cling to the tenderloins and brought needed richness to the lean proteins as well as plenty of herbal flavor. In the circulated heat of the air fryer, the meat cooked evenly even without flipping and the prosciutto crisped up. A spritz of fresh lemon added pleasant brightness to our perfectly cooked tenderloins.

2 (1-pound) pork tenderloins, trimmed and halved crosswise

6 tablespoons unsalted butter, melted

¼ teaspoon pepper

12 thin slices prosciutto (6 ounces)

8 large fresh sage leaves

Lemon wedges

1 Pat pork dry with paper towels, brush with 3 tablespoons melted butter, and season with pepper. For each piece of pork, shingle 3 slices of prosciutto on cutting board, overlapping edges slightly, and lay pork in center. (Tuck thinner tail ends of tenderloins under themselves as needed to create uniform bundles.) Top with 2 sage leaves, then fold prosciutto around pork, pressing on overlapping ends to secure. Brush pork bundles with remaining 3 tablespoons melted butter and arrange seam side down in air-fryer basket.

2 Place basket in air fryer and set temperature to 400 degrees. Cook until pork registers 140 degrees, 20 to 25 minutes. Transfer pork to cutting board, tent with aluminum foil, and let rest for 5 minutes. Slice pork ½ inch thick and serve with lemon wedges.

SWEET AND SMOKY PORK TENDERLOIN WITH ROASTED BUTTERNUT SQUASH

Serves 2

COOK TIME 24 minutes   **TOTAL TIME** 1 hour

why this recipe works A hearty, autumnal meal of roast pork and butternut squash can require hours in the oven. But by carefully arranging the ingredients in our air-fryer basket, we produced dinner for two in just an hour, with little more than the basket to wash. A 1-pound pork tenderloin proved to be the right size. After cutting it in half, we tossed it in a mixture of molasses, garlic, and smoked paprika, giving it smokiness, sweetness, and deep color, before placing it atop a roasting pile of cubed butternut squash that we'd jump-started in the air fryer. A bonus: The smoky molasses glaze dripped down onto the squash during cooking, creating beautifully caramelized, tasty edges. For a final burst of flavor and texture, we tossed the squash with roasted pepitas, butter, a touch more molasses, lime zest, and lime juice and sprinkled on minced chives. You can roast pepitas in the air fryer; see page 13.

1¼ pounds butternut squash, peeled, seeded, and cut into ¾-inch pieces (5 cups)

1 tablespoon unsalted butter, melted

Salt and pepper

3½ teaspoons molasses

1 teaspoon smoked paprika

1 garlic clove, minced

1 (1-pound) pork tenderloin, trimmed and halved crosswise

1 teaspoon grated lime zest plus 1 teaspoon juice

2 tablespoons roasted pepitas

1 tablespoon minced fresh chives

1 Toss squash with 1½ teaspoons melted butter, ⅛ teaspoon salt, and ⅛ teaspoon pepper in large bowl; transfer to air-fryer basket. Place basket in air fryer and set temperature to 350 degrees. Cook squash for 8 minutes, tossing halfway through cooking.

2 Meanwhile, microwave 3 teaspoons molasses, paprika, garlic, ½ teaspoon salt, and ½ teaspoon pepper in now-empty bowl until fragrant, about 30 seconds, stirring halfway through microwaving. Pat pork dry with paper towels, add to molasses mixture, and toss to coat.

3 Stir squash, then arrange tenderloin pieces on top. (Tuck thinner tail end of tenderloin under itself as needed to create uniform pieces.) Return basket to air fryer and cook until pork registers 140 degrees, 16 to 21 minutes, flipping and rotating tenderloin pieces halfway through cooking. Transfer pork to large plate, tent with aluminum foil, and let rest while finishing squash.

4 Whisk lime zest and juice, remaining ½ teaspoon molasses, and remaining 1½ teaspoons melted butter together in medium bowl. Add squash, pepitas, and chives and toss to coat. Season with salt and pepper to taste. Slice pork ½ inch thick and serve with squash.

VIETNAMESE-STYLE RICE NOODLE SALAD WITH PORK

Serves 4

COOK TIME 16 minutes   **TOTAL TIME** 50 minutes

why this recipe works This aromatic salad is light but multilayered, composed of juicy roast pork tenderloin, crisp vegetables, fresh herbs, and thin rice noodles. The air fryer offered a hands-off way to roast the pork and gave us perfectly cooked results. To create bold flavors, we briefly marinated the pork in ginger, fish sauce, sugar, and chili-garlic sauce before roasting it, then we used the same seasonings plus lime juice to build a bright dressing for the noodles. While the cooked pork rested, we set up our noodle bowls, slicing the pork thinly and laying it on the noodles along with cucumber, carrot, mint, and chopped peanuts.

2 tablespoons fish sauce	1 teaspoon vegetable oil	1 carrot, peeled and grated
1 tablespoon grated fresh ginger	1 (1-pound) pork tenderloin, trimmed and halved crosswise	½ seedless cucumber, cut into 2-inch-long matchsticks
1 tablespoon packed brown sugar	8 ounces rice vermicelli	2 tablespoons dry-roasted peanuts, chopped
1½ teaspoons Asian chili-garlic sauce	¼ cup lime juice (2 limes), plus lime wedges for serving	2 teaspoons chopped fresh mint

1 Whisk 1 teaspoon fish sauce, 1½ teaspoons ginger, 1 teaspoon sugar, ½ teaspoon chili-garlic sauce, and oil together in large bowl. Pat pork dry with paper towels, add to fish sauce mixture, and toss to coat. Arrange pork in air-fryer basket, spaced evenly apart. (Tuck thinner tail end of tenderloin under itself as needed to create uniform piece.) Place basket in air fryer and set temperature to 350 degrees. Cook until pork registers 140 degrees, 16 to 21 minutes, flipping and rotating tenderloin pieces halfway through cooking. Transfer pork to carving board, tent with aluminum foil, and let rest while preparing noodles.

2 Place noodles in separate large bowl and pour 6 cups boiling water over top. Stir noodles briefly to ensure they are completely submerged, then let soak, stirring occasionally, until tender, about 2 minutes. Drain noodles, rinse under cold water, then drain well again; set aside.

3 Whisk lime juice, remaining 5 teaspoons fish sauce, remaining 1½ teaspoons ginger, remaining 2 teaspoons sugar, and remaining 1 teaspoon chili-garlic sauce in separate bowl until sugar has dissolved. Slice pork ½ inch thick. Divide noodles among individual serving bowls and top with pork, carrot, and cucumber. Whisk any accumulated pork juices into sauce and drizzle over each bowl. Sprinkle with peanuts and mint. Serve with lime wedges.

POLYNESIAN PORK KEBABS WITH PINEAPPLE AND ONION

Serves 2

COOK TIME 17 minutes   **TOTAL TIME** 1 hour

why this recipe works Combining meaty boneless country-style pork ribs with pineapple and peppers and onions gives our kebabs a Polynesian flavor. We marinated the pork briefly in a blend of garlic, ginger, red pepper flakes, soy sauce, and ketchup, which gave our marinade sweetness and helped it to cling to the pork. We also added a couple of pineapple pieces and mashed them to give our marinade pineapple flavor without opening a can of pineapple juice. So that everything cooked evenly and finished at the same time, we skewered the vegetables and fruit first, giving them a head start in the air fryer before placing our pork skewers on top. At the meat counter, country-style ribs can have widely varying proportions of light and dark meat; be sure to choose those with a greater amount of dark.

- 2 tablespoons extra-virgin olive oil
- 2 garlic cloves, minced
- 1½ teaspoons grated fresh ginger
- ¼ teaspoon red pepper flakes
- 1½ cups 1-inch pineapple pieces

- 2 tablespoons ketchup
- 4 teaspoons soy sauce
- 2 teaspoons packed brown sugar
- 12 ounces boneless country-style pork ribs, trimmed and cut into 1½-inch pieces

- 1 red bell pepper, stemmed, seeded, and cut into 1½-inch pieces
- 1 small red onion, halved and cut through root end into 6 equal wedges
- Salt and pepper
- 5 (6-inch) wooden skewers

1 Microwave 4 teaspoons oil, garlic, ginger, and pepper flakes in large bowl until fragrant, about 30 seconds, stirring once halfway through. Add 2 pineapple pieces and mash with fork until mostly smooth. Stir in ketchup, soy sauce, and sugar. Add pork and toss to coat; set aside.

2 Toss remaining pineapple, bell pepper, and onion with remaining 2 teaspoons oil in separate bowl and season with salt and pepper. Thread 1 piece of onion onto wooden skewer. Thread one-third of pineapple and bell pepper onto skewer, followed by second piece of onion. Repeat skewering remaining vegetables and pineapple with 2 more

skewers. Arrange skewers in air-fryer basket, parallel to each other and spaced evenly apart. Place basket in air fryer, set temperature to 400 degrees, and cook for 5 minutes.

3 Meanwhile, thread pork evenly onto remaining 2 skewers. Flip and rotate pineapple-vegetable skewers, then arrange pork skewers on top, perpendicular to pineapple-vegetable skewers. Return basket to air fryer and cook until pork registers 140 degrees and vegetables are crisp-tender, 12 to 16 minutes, flipping and rotating pork skewers halfway through cooking. Serve.

ITALIAN SAUSAGE AND PEPPER SUBS

Serves 4

COOK TIME 24 minutes   **TOTAL TIME** 50 minutes

why this recipe works Appearing everywhere from ballparks to street fairs, Italian sausage subs stuffed with sweet peppers and onions offer a fun meal—one that's especially easy to make at home in an air fryer. Less fussy than grilling, the air fryer was similarly able to crisp and brown all the ingredients at once, while allowing excess fat to drip away. Since the peppers and onions needed more time to cook, we gave them a jump start, using that time to brush our sausages with a little honey, which improved browning and added pleasant sweetness. We stacked our sausages right on top of our onions and peppers, flipping them after a few minutes to give one side deep browning we thought was achievable only with a grill. For a quick accompaniment, a combination of whole-grain mustard, mayonnaise, and red wine vinegar balanced the richness of the sausage and gave our sandwiches a pop of flavor. Warming the honey makes it easier to brush onto the sausages.

2 red or green bell peppers, stemmed, seeded, and cut into ¼-inch-wide strips	**Pepper**	1 tablespoon mayonnaise
	1 pound hot or sweet Italian sausage (6 sausages)	1 teaspoon red wine vinegar
1 onion, halved and sliced ¼ inch thick	2 teaspoons honey, warmed	½ teaspoon sugar
2 teaspoons vegetable oil	2 tablespoons whole-grain mustard	4 (6-inch) Italian sub rolls, split lengthwise

1 Toss bell peppers and onion with oil and ¼ teaspoon pepper in bowl; transfer to air-fryer basket. Place basket in air fryer, set temperature to 350 degrees, and cook for 8 minutes.

2 Brush sausages with honey. Stir peppers and onion, then arrange sausages on top, spaced evenly apart. Return basket to air fryer and cook until vegetables are tender and sausages are lightly browned and register 160 degrees, 16 to 18 minutes, flipping and rotating sausages and stirring vegetables once after 5 minutes.

3 Transfer sausages to cutting board, tent with aluminum foil, and let rest for 5 minutes. Whisk mustard, mayonnaise, vinegar, sugar, and ¼ teaspoon pepper together in bowl. Halve sausages crosswise on bias. Divide sausages, peppers, and onion evenly among rolls and drizzle with mustard sauce. Serve.

MUSTARD-THYME LAMB CHOPS WITH ROASTED CARROTS

Serves 2

COOK TIME 24 minutes   **TOTAL TIME** 40 minutes

why this recipe works Lean, tender, mildly flavored lamb loin chops are a good fit for the air fryer, which can easily hold four of these "mini T-bones." To take advantage of the air fryer's circulated heat, we roasted them atop a side of carrots, coating both with a glaze of mustard, honey, garlic, lemon zest and juice, and fresh thyme. But while the carrots emerged irresistibly tender and caramelized and the lamb was perfectly pink, the exterior of the chops lacked color. We suspected the moisture in our glaze prevented the lamb from browning during its quick roast. Instead, brushing the chops with oil and honey before cooking and dabbing on the mustard mixture after gave us the best of both worlds—browned chops accented with a fragrant and flavorful glaze. If your lamb chops are smaller than 6 ounces, you may need to continue cooking the carrots in step 2 after the chops are done. Warming the honey makes it easier to brush onto the lamb.

- 1 pound carrots, peeled and cut into 2-inch lengths, thick ends halved lengthwise
- 4 teaspoons extra-virgin olive oil
- Salt and pepper
- 1 tablespoon honey, warmed
- 4 (6-ounce) lamb loin chops, 1 ¼ inches thick, trimmed
- 1 tablespoon Dijon mustard
- 1½ teaspoons minced fresh thyme
- 1 garlic clove, minced
- 1 teaspoon grated lemon zest plus 1 teaspoon juice
- 1 teaspoon water

1 Toss carrots with 1 teaspoon oil, ⅛ teaspoon salt, and ⅛ teaspoon pepper in bowl; transfer to air-fryer basket. Place basket in air fryer, set temperature to 350 degrees, and cook for 14 minutes, stirring halfway through cooking.

2 Combine 2 teaspoons honey and 2 teaspoons oil in small bowl. Pat chops dry with paper towels, brush with honey-oil mixture, and season with salt and pepper. Stir carrots, then arrange chops on top, spaced evenly apart. Return basket to air fryer and cook until chops are lightly browned and register 120 to 125 degrees (for medium-rare) or 130 to 135 degrees (for medium), 10 to 15 minutes, flipping and rotating chops halfway through cooking.

3 Microwave mustard, thyme, garlic, lemon zest and juice, water, remaining 1 teaspoon oil, and remaining 1 teaspoon honey in medium bowl until fragrant, about 30 seconds, stirring once halfway through. Transfer chops to plate and brush with 1 tablespoon of mustard mixture. Tent with aluminum foil and let rest while finishing carrots.

4 Transfer carrots to bowl with remaining mustard mixture and toss to coat. Season with salt and pepper to taste. Serve lamb with carrots.

LAMB SLIDERS WITH APRICOT CHUTNEY

Serves 2

COOK TIME 9 minutes   **TOTAL TIME** 40 minutes

why this recipe works Sliders should be fun, and part of the fun comes from playing with a variety of flavorings and toppings, as in this supereasy version, which translates the fantastic combo of rich lamb, fragrant rosemary, and sweet-tart apricot chutney into a miniature burger. The lamb patties needed minimal attention when cooked in the air fryer. Meanwhile, we devised a brilliantly simple chutney using dried apricots, a chopped shallot, brown sugar, rosemary, and lemon juice, which cooked in just a minute in the microwave. Goat cheese and baby arugula required zero prep and provided tanginess and a peppery bite to cut the richness of the lamb. Coming together in just 40 minutes, our elegant and attractive sliders make a fun appetizer or an easy and unique weeknight meal for two. You can toast rolls in your air fryer; see page 13.

10 ounces ground lamb	2 tablespoons water	1 teaspoon lemon juice
½ teaspoon garlic powder	1 small shallot, chopped fine	1 ounce goat cheese, crumbled (¼ cup)
Salt and pepper	2 teaspoons packed brown sugar	4 soft white dinner rolls or slider buns, toasted if desired
2 tablespoons finely chopped dried apricots	1½ teaspoons minced fresh rosemary or ½ teaspoon dried	¾ cup baby arugula

1 Divide lamb into 4 lightly packed balls, then gently flatten each into ½-inch-thick patties. Press center of each patty with fingertips to create ¼-inch-deep depression. Sprinkle with garlic powder and season with salt and pepper.

2 Arrange patties in air-fryer basket, spaced evenly apart. Place basket in air fryer and set temperature to 400 degrees. Cook until sliders are lightly browned and register 160 degrees, about 9 minutes, flipping and rotating sliders halfway through cooking.

3 Meanwhile, microwave apricots, water, shallot, sugar, rosemary, lemon juice, and pinch salt in bowl until apricots soften, about 1 minute. Using fork, mash apricots against side of bowl to thicken chutney.

4 Transfer sliders to plate and top with goat cheese. Spread 2 teaspoons chutney on each roll bottom, top with sliders and arugula, then cap with roll tops. Serve.

LAMB SLIDERS WITH SMOKY TOMATO RELISH

Omit sugar and lemon juice. Substitute oil-packed sun-dried tomatoes, patted dry and finely chopped, for apricots, ⅛ teaspoon smoked paprika for rosemary, feta cheese for goat cheese, and baby spinach for arugula.

LAMB KOFTE WRAPS

Serves 2

COOK TIME 10 minutes   **TOTAL TIME** 40 minutes

why this recipe works Found throughout the Middle East, North Africa, the eastern Mediterranean, and Asia, *kofte* come in a variety of shapes—patties, balls, or cigars—and are made from ground lamb or beef flavored with spices and fresh herbs. We were looking to create an easy air-fryer version that mimicked the cigar-shaped lamb kofte that are formed around skewers and grilled, but without the need for skewers and tending to a grill. The kofte's cylindrical shape lent itself to being wrapped in pita bread as a sandwich and also fit well in the confines of the air-fryer basket. A quick mixture of Greek yogurt, fresh mint, lemon juice, and garlic did double duty: providing moisture and flavor to the ground lamb, and serving as a base for shredded cucumber to make a cooling and tangy tzatziki sauce to dollop on our sandwiches. At 400 degrees, the kofte cooked quickly in the circulated hot air, staying tender and juicy, but we found that to ensure even cooking without breaking the kofte apart, we needed to rotate them slightly past the halfway point, when they were firmer and more easily handled. Folded in pita breads with minty tzatziki, crisp shredded lettuce, slices of sharp red onion, and juicy tomato, our air-fryer kofte wraps were complete.

½ cup plain Greek yogurt

4 teaspoons minced fresh mint

2 teaspoons lemon juice

1 garlic clove, minced

   Salt and pepper

10 ounces ground lamb

¼ English cucumber, shredded (¼ cup)

1 small tomato, cored, halved, and sliced thin

¼ cup thinly sliced red onion

1 cup shredded iceberg lettuce

2 (8-inch) pita breads

1 Whisk yogurt, mint, lemon juice, garlic, ¼ teaspoon salt, and ⅛ teaspoon pepper in medium bowl until well combined. Transfer 2 tablespoons yogurt mixture to separate medium bowl; set remaining yogurt mixture aside. Break up ground lamb into small pieces over yogurt mixture and add ⅛ teaspoon salt and ⅛ teaspoon pepper. Lightly knead with hands until well combined. Divide mixture into 4 lightly packed balls, then shape into 5-inch cylinders.

2 Arrange kofte in air-fryer basket, spaced evenly apart. Place basket in air fryer and set temperature to 400 degrees. Cook until kofte are lightly browned and register 160 degrees, about 10 minutes, flipping and rotating kofte after 7 minutes of cooking.

3 Stir cucumber into reserved yogurt sauce and season with salt and pepper to taste. Arrange kofte, tomato, onion, and lettuce evenly over each pita and dollop each wrap with 2 tablespoons tzatziki. Serve, passing remaining tzatziki separately.

LAMB MEATBALLS WITH COUSCOUS

Serves 2

COOK TIME 13 minutes   **TOTAL TIME** 40 minutes

why this recipe works Grain bowls—cooked grains topped with proteins, vegetables, and usually a sauce and garnish—are a go-to weeknight meal, satisfying and hearty. But they shouldn't be a lot of work. With its hands-off convenience, speed, and easy cleanup, the air fryer promised an easier route to building a bowl without requiring any pots or pans. We mixed up some succulent lamb meatballs and popped them into the basket to cook while we pulled together a base of couscous, which we softened in a mixture of water and orange juice for a sweetness and an aroma that paired perfectly with the lamb. A mixture of yogurt, garlic, and fresh dill seasoned the meatballs and added moisture and tang; a few warm spices rounded out the flavors. The same yogurt mixture doubled as a sauce, so we made plenty to drizzle over our bowls. To bring color, crunch, and some vegetables to the dish, we tossed in grated carrots as well as chopped raisins, and sprinkled on toasted almonds and additional chopped dill. You can toast the almonds in your air fryer; see page 13.

⅔ cup plain yogurt

2½ tablespoons minced fresh dill

1 garlic clove, minced

Salt and pepper

10 ounces ground lamb

½ teaspoon ground cumin

¼ teaspoon ground cinnamon

¼ cup water

¼ teaspoon grated orange zest plus ¼ cup juice

½ cup couscous

2 tablespoons chopped raisins

¼ cup shredded carrot

2 tablespoons chopped toasted almonds

1 Whisk yogurt, 1 tablespoon dill, garlic, ¼ teaspoon salt, and ⅛ teaspoon pepper in bowl until well combined. Transfer 2 tablespoons yogurt sauce to medium bowl; set remaining yogurt sauce aside for serving. Break up ground lamb into small pieces over yogurt mixture and add cumin, cinnamon, ⅛ teaspoon salt, and ⅛ teaspoon pepper. Lightly knead with hands until well combined. Pinch off and roll mixture into 6 meatballs.

2 Arrange meatballs in air-fryer basket, spaced evenly apart. Place basket in air fryer and set temperature to 400 degrees. Cook meatballs until lightly browned and register 160 degrees, 13 to 14 minutes, rotating meat-balls after 10 minutes.

3 Meanwhile, combine water and orange juice in large bowl and microwave until boiling, 3 to 5 minutes. Stir in couscous, raisins, orange zest, and ⅛ teaspoon salt. Cover and let sit until couscous is tender and all liquid has been absorbed, about 7 minutes. Add carrot and 1 tablespoon dill and gently fluff with fork to combine.

4 Divide couscous between individual serving bowls and top with meatballs. Sprinkle with almonds and remaining 1½ teaspoons dill and serve with reserved yogurt sauce.

SEAFOOD

BETTER-THAN-BOXED FISH STICKS

Makes about 20 fish sticks; serves 4

COOK TIME 10 minutes   **TOTAL TIME** 1 hour, plus freezing time

why this recipe works Don't settle for bland, dried-out supermarket fish sticks. Making your own as a freezer staple guarantees fresh fish and a flavorful coating anytime, and the air fryer can cook a serving faster than it takes the oven to preheat. Meaty haddock stood up to a crunchy coating and held its shape during cooking. Brining the fish briefly ensured it stayed moist and well seasoned after freezing, and a generous addition of Old Bay seasoning in the coating brought classic flavors. You can substitute halibut or cod for the haddock. For the crispiest fish sticks, cook one serving at a time, respraying the basket between batches. You can also cook fish sticks without freezing; reduce the cooking time to 8 to 10 minutes. Serve with Tartar Sauce or Old Bay Dipping sauce.

Salt and pepper

1½ pounds skinless haddock fillets, ¾ inch thick, sliced into 4-inch strips

2 cups panko bread crumbs

1 tablespoon vegetable oil

¼ cup all-purpose flour

¼ cup mayonnaise

2 large eggs

2 tablespoons Dijon mustard

1 tablespoon Old Bay seasoning

1 Dissolve ¼ cup salt in 2 quarts cold water in large container. Add haddock, cover, and let sit for 15 minutes.

2 Toss panko with oil in bowl until evenly coated. Microwave, stirring frequently, until light golden brown, 2 to 4 minutes; transfer to shallow dish. Whisk flour, mayonnaise, eggs, mustard, Old Bay, ⅛ teaspoon salt, and ⅛ teaspoon pepper together in second shallow dish.

3 Set wire rack in rimmed baking sheet and spray with vegetable oil spray. Remove haddock from brine and thoroughly pat dry with paper towels. Working with 1 piece at a time, dredge haddock in egg mixture, letting excess drip off, then coat with panko mixture, pressing gently to adhere. Transfer fish sticks to prepared rack and freeze until firm, about 1 hour. (Frozen fish sticks can be transferred to zipper-lock bag and stored in freezer for up to 1 month; do not thaw before cooking.)

4 to cook fish sticks Lightly spray base of air-fryer basket with vegetable oil spray. Arrange up to 5 fish sticks in prepared basket, spaced evenly apart. Place basket in air fryer and set temperature to 400 degrees. Cook until fish sticks are golden and register 140 degrees, 10 to 12 minutes, flipping and rotating fish sticks halfway through cooking. Serve.

TARTAR SAUCE
Whisk ¼ cup plain Greek yogurt, 2 tablespoons mayonnaise, 2 tablespoons dill pickle relish, ¾ teaspoon distilled white vinegar, ¼ teaspoon Worcestershire sauce, ¼ teaspoon pepper, and pinch salt together in bowl.

OLD BAY DIPPING SAUCE
Whisk ¼ cup plain Greek yogurt, 2 tablespoons mayonnaise, 1½ teaspoons Dijon mustard, and ¾ teaspoon Old Bay seasoning together in bowl. Season with salt and pepper to taste.

CRUNCHY AIR-FRIED COD FILLETS

Serves 2

COOK TIME 12 minutes   **TOTAL TIME** 45 minutes

why this recipe works Fish is so moist that any attempt to give it a crisp crust (short of deep frying) is likely to end up soggy, especially on the underside. Rather than fight this, we didn't try to bread the fish all over but instead simply pressed pretoasted panko crumbs onto the top, which streamlined the process and still gave us crunch in every bite. A coating of mayonnaise, egg yolk, and lemon zest boosted flavor and helped the crumbs adhere. But even with our streamlined breading, the flaky cod was too delicate to lift from the air-fryer basket without breaking. A foil sling came to the rescue, enabling us to rotate and later remove the fillets in one piece. You can substitute halibut or haddock for the cod. For more information on making a foil sling, see page 11. Serve with Creamy Chipotle Chile Sauce, if desired.

- ⅓ cup panko bread crumbs
- 1 teaspoon vegetable oil
- 1 small shallot, minced
- 1 small garlic clove, minced
- ½ teaspoon minced fresh thyme or ⅛ teaspoon dried
- Salt and pepper
- 1 tablespoon minced fresh parsley
- 1 tablespoon mayonnaise
- 1 large egg yolk
- ¼ teaspoon grated lemon zest, plus lemon wedges for serving
- 2 (8-ounce) skinless cod fillets, 1¼ inches thick

1 Make foil sling for air-fryer basket by folding 1 long sheet of aluminum foil so it is 4 inches wide. Lay sheet of foil widthwise across basket, pressing foil into and up sides of basket. Fold excess foil as needed so that edges of foil are flush with top of basket. Lightly spray foil and basket with vegetable oil spray.

2 Toss panko with oil in bowl until evenly coated. Stir in shallot, garlic, thyme, ¼ teaspoon salt, and ⅛ teaspoon pepper. Microwave, stirring frequently, until panko is light golden brown, about 2 minutes. Transfer to shallow dish and let cool slightly; stir in parsley. Whisk mayonnaise, egg yolk, lemon zest, and ⅛ teaspoon pepper together in bowl.

3 Pat cod dry with paper towels and season with salt and pepper. Arrange fillets skinned side down on plate and brush tops evenly with mayonnaise mixture. (Tuck thinner tail ends of fillets under themselves as needed to create uniform pieces.) Working with 1 fillet at a time, dredge coated side in panko mixture, pressing gently to adhere. Arrange fillets crumb side up on sling in prepared basket, spaced evenly apart. Place basket in air fryer and set temperature to 300 degrees. Cook until cod registers 140 degrees, 12 to 16 minutes, using sling to rotate fillets halfway through cooking. Using sling, carefully remove cod from air fryer. Serve with lemon wedges.

CREAMY CHIPOTLE CHILE SAUCE

Whisk ¼ cup mayonnaise, ¼ cup sour cream, 2 teaspoons minced canned chipotle chile in adobo sauce, 1 small minced garlic clove, 2 teaspoons minced fresh cilantro, and 1 teaspoon lime juice together in bowl.

ROASTED COD WITH LEMON-GARLIC POTATOES

Serves 2

COOK TIME 28 minutes	TOTAL TIME 1 hour

why this recipe works The air fryer excels at cooking both crispy potatoes and moist, flaky fish, and this elegantly simple recipe combines both into an easy dinner for two. Thinly slicing a russet potato and shingling it not only made an attractive bed for the fish but also helped it to cook faster. We tossed the slices with melted butter, garlic, and lemon zest, arranged them in two layers on a foil sling for easy removal, then roasted them until they turned tender and spotty brown before laying cod fillets on top and letting both cook together. A pat of lemon-herb compound butter and lemon slices basted the fish with flavor as it cooked. Soon we had a perfect dinner of subtly flavored cod and fragrant potatoes. You can substitute halibut or haddock for the cod. For more information on making a foil sling, see page 11.

3 tablespoons unsalted butter, softened

2 garlic cloves, minced

1 lemon, grated to yield 2 teaspoons zest and sliced ¼ inch thick

Salt and pepper

1 large russet potato (12 ounces), unpeeled, sliced ¼ inch thick

1 tablespoon minced fresh parsley, chives, or tarragon

2 (8-ounce) skinless cod fillets, 1¼ inches thick

1 Make foil sling for air-fryer basket by folding 1 long sheet of aluminum foil so it is 4 inches wide. Lay sheet of foil widthwise across basket, pressing foil into and up sides of basket. Fold excess foil as needed so that edges of foil are flush with top of basket. Lightly spray foil and basket with vegetable oil spray.

2 Microwave 1 tablespoon butter, garlic, 1 teaspoon lemon zest, ¼ teaspoon salt, and ⅛ teaspoon pepper in medium bowl, stirring once, until butter is melted and mixture is fragrant, about 30 seconds. Add potato slices and toss to coat. Shingle potato slices on sling in prepared basket to create 2 even layers. Place basket in air fryer and set temperature to 400 degrees. Cook until potato slices are spotty brown and just tender, 16 to 18 minutes, using sling to rotate potatoes halfway through cooking.

3 Combine remaining 2 tablespoons butter, remaining 1 teaspoon lemon zest, and parsley in small bowl. Pat cod dry with paper towels and season with salt and pepper. Place fillets skinned side down on top of potato slices, spaced evenly apart. (Tuck thinner tail ends of fillets under themselves as needed to create uniform pieces.) Dot fillets with butter mixture and top with lemon slices. Return basket to air fryer and cook until cod flakes apart when gently prodded with paring knife and registers 140 degrees, 12 to 15 minutes, using sling to rotate potato slices and cod halfway through cooking.

4 Using sling, carefully remove potatoes and cod from air fryer. Cut potato slices into 2 portions between fillets using fish spatula. Slide spatula along underside of potato slices and transfer with cod to individual plates. Serve.

MOROCCAN SPICED HALIBUT WITH CHICKPEA SALAD

Serves 2

COOK TIME 12 minutes   **TOTAL TIME** 35 minutes

why this recipe works For an adventurous twist on a fish dinner, we turned to the flavors of North Africa. Rubbing halibut fillets with coriander, cumin, ginger, and cinnamon gave them a warm, fragrant flavor and aroma, and the air fryer cooked them gently and evenly, producing moist and tender fillets. Meanwhile, we made a quick Moroccan chickpea and carrot salad. Warming the chickpeas helped their skins to break down and absorb more dressing, avoiding a lackluster salad. A touch of honey complemented the carrots' sweetness, harissa added heat and complexity, and a sprinkling of mint offered a cooling note and pretty splash of green. You can substitute cod or haddock for the halibut. If harissa is unavailable, it can be omitted. For more information on making a foil sling, see page 11.

¾ teaspoon ground coriander

½ teaspoon ground cumin

¼ teaspoon ground ginger

⅛ teaspoon ground cinnamon

Salt and pepper

2 (8-ounce) skinless halibut fillets, 1¼ inches thick

4 teaspoons extra-virgin olive oil, plus extra for drizzling

1 (15-ounce) can chickpeas, rinsed

1 tablespoon lemon juice, plus lemon wedges for serving

1 teaspoon harissa

½ teaspoon honey

2 carrots, peeled and shredded

2 tablespoons chopped fresh mint

1 Make foil sling for air-fryer basket by folding 1 long sheet of aluminum foil so it is 4 inches wide. Lay sheet of foil widthwise across basket, pressing foil into and up sides of basket. Fold excess foil as needed so that edges of foil are flush with top of basket. Lightly spray foil and basket with vegetable oil spray.

2 Combine coriander, cumin, ginger, cinnamon, ⅛ teaspoon salt, and ⅛ teaspoon pepper in small bowl. Pat halibut dry with paper towels, rub with 1 teaspoon oil, and sprinkle all over with spice mixture. Arrange fillets skinned side down on sling in prepared basket, spaced evenly apart. Place basket in air fryer and set temperature to 300 degrees.

Cook until halibut flakes apart when gently prodded with paring knife and registers 140 degrees, 12 to 16 minutes, using sling to rotate fillets halfway through cooking.

3 Meanwhile, microwave chickpeas in medium bowl until heated through, about 2 minutes. Stir in remaining 1 tablespoon oil, lemon juice, harissa, honey, ⅛ teaspoon salt, and ⅛ teaspoon pepper. Add carrots and 1 tablespoon mint and toss to combine. Season with salt and pepper to taste.

4 Using sling, carefully remove halibut from air fryer and transfer to individual plates. Sprinkle with remaining 1 tablespoon mint and drizzle with extra oil to taste. Serve with salad and lemon wedges.

SOLE AND ASPARAGUS BUNDLES WITH TARRAGON BUTTER

Serves 2

COOK TIME 14 minutes   **TOTAL TIME** 40 minutes

why this recipe works Mild, creamy sole is delicious but tricky to cook, as the long, delicate fillets easily fall apart. One solution: sole bundles. Rolled around a filling into a tidy package, the fish is easier to maneuver and is perfectly shaped for the air fryer. For the filling, we chose asparagus, which was easy to prep and made for an attractive presentation. To ensure the spears became tender as the fish finished cooking, we steamed them in the microwave before rolling them in the fillets. Placing the bundles on a foil sling made transferring them easy, and rubbing them with oil kept the fillets from sticking to each other. To flavor the mild, lean fish, we dotted the bundles with a compound butter made with tarragon, minced shallot, and lemon zest and juice when they came out of the fryer. Served with a salad or grain, this is a light and sophisticated dinner for two. Look for asparagus spears that are about ½ inch thick. For more information on making a foil sling, see page 11.

8   ounces asparagus, trimmed

1   teaspoon extra-virgin olive oil

Salt and pepper

4   (3-ounce) skinless sole or flounder fillets, ⅛ to ¼ inch thick

4   tablespoons unsalted butter, softened

1   small shallot, minced

1   tablespoon chopped fresh tarragon

¼   teaspoon lemon zest plus ½ teaspoon juice

1 Toss asparagus with ½ teaspoon oil, pinch salt, and pinch pepper in bowl. Cover and microwave until bright green and just tender, about 3 minutes, tossing halfway through microwaving. Uncover and set aside to cool slightly.

2 Make foil sling for air-fryer basket by folding 1 long sheet of aluminum foil so it is 4 inches wide. Lay sheet of foil widthwise across basket, pressing foil into and up sides of basket. Fold excess foil as needed so that edges of foil are flush with top of basket. Lightly spray foil and basket with vegetable oil spray.

3 Pat sole dry with paper towels and season with salt and pepper. Arrange fillets skinned side up on cutting board, with thicker ends closest to you. Arrange asparagus evenly across base of each fillet, then tightly roll fillets away from you around asparagus to form tidy bundles.

4 Rub bundles evenly with remaining ½ teaspoon oil and arrange seam side down on sling in prepared basket. Place basket in air fryer and set temperature to 300 degrees. Cook until asparagus is tender and sole flakes apart when gently prodded with paring knife, 14 to 18 minutes, using sling to rotate bundles halfway through cooking.

5 Combine butter, shallot, tarragon, and lemon zest and juice in bowl. Using sling, carefully remove sole bundles from air fryer and transfer to individual plates. Top evenly with butter mixture and serve.

ROASTED SALMON FILLETS

Serves 2

COOK TIME 10 minutes   **TOTAL TIME** 25 minutes

why this recipe works The air fryer proved to be an excellent way to cook salmon. Testers couldn't stop raving about how the method was easier and less messy than using a skillet, and they loved that they didn't have to closely monitor the fish to avoid overcooking it, thanks to the air fryer's built-in timer and controlled temperature. And the results were great: moist, flaky fish with a beautifully bronzed exterior. Cooking the fish at 400 degrees gave us the best color but also created a problem: smoke, which came from the salmon's delicious fat dripping to the bottom as well as splattering onto the heating element above. Since the fat primarily resides in the skin, we cooked the fillets skin side down, away from the heating element, and used a foil sling, which prevented fat from dripping to the bottom. (Bonus: Our fillets were also now easier to rotate and to remove.) If using wild salmon, cook it until it registers 120 degrees. For more information on making a foil sling, see page 11. Serve with Herb-Yogurt Sauce or Mango-Mint Salsa.

2 (8-ounce) skin-on salmon fillets, 1½ inches thick

1 teaspoon vegetable oil

Salt and pepper

1 Make foil sling for air-fryer basket by folding 1 long sheet of aluminum foil so it is 4 inches wide. Lay sheet of foil widthwise across basket, pressing foil into and up sides of basket. Fold excess foil as needed so that edges of foil are flush with top of basket. Lightly spray foil and basket with vegetable oil spray.

2 Pat salmon dry with paper towels, rub with oil, and season with salt and pepper. Arrange fillets skin side down on sling in prepared basket, spaced evenly apart. Place basket in air fryer and set temperature to 400 degrees. Cook salmon until center is still translucent when checked with tip of paring knife and registers 125 degrees (for medium-rare), 10 to 14 minutes, using sling to rotate fillets halfway through cooking.

3 Using sling, carefully remove salmon from air fryer. Slide fish spatula along underside of fillets and transfer to individual serving plates, leaving skin behind. Serve.

HERB-YOGURT SAUCE
Combine ½ cup plain yogurt, 2 tablespoons minced fresh dill or tarragon, ½ teaspoon grated lemon zest plus 2 teaspoons juice, and 1 small minced garlic clove in bowl. Season with salt and pepper to taste. Cover and refrigerate until flavors meld, about 30 minutes. Makes about ½ cup.

MANGO-MINT SALSA
Combine 1 peeled, pitted, and finely chopped mango, 1 small seeded and minced jalapeño chile, 3 tablespoons lime juice (2 limes), 2 tablespoons chopped fresh mint, 1 tablespoon minced shallot, 1 tablespoon extra-virgin olive oil, and ¼ teaspoon salt in bowl. Makes about 1½ cups.

ORANGE-MUSTARD GLAZED SALMON

Serves 2

COOK TIME 10 minutes   **TOTAL TIME** 30 minutes

why this recipe works A sweet, tangy glaze offers appealing contrast to rich, meaty salmon but most recipes stumble by calling for broiling the fish, which can result in unevenly cooked salmon and a burnt glaze. So we were happy to find the air fryer produced foolproof results; the direct heat from above caramelized the glaze's sugars, while the circulated air cooked the fish from all sides. We liked the idea of an orange glaze, but on their own orange juice and zest didn't pack enough punch. Adding orange marmalade was just the ticket to boost the flavor, and it helped the glaze cling to the salmon. Some whole-grain mustard gave the glaze more acidity and pops of mild heat to balance its sweetness and cut the richness of the fish. We brushed the mixture on the fillets before cooking and after 10 minutes were met with crisp-glazed fish boasting beautiful browned edges and a velvety pink interior. This easy technique lends itself to a variety of flavors, so we also developed a honey-chipotle glaze and an Asian-inspired glaze made with hoisin and rice vinegar. If using wild salmon, cook it until it registers 120 degrees. For more information on making a foil sling, see page 11.

1 tablespoon orange marmalade	2 teaspoons whole-grain mustard	Salt and pepper
¼ teaspoon grated orange zest plus 1 tablespoon juice	2 (8-ounce) skin-on salmon fillets, 1 ½ inches thick	

1 Make foil sling for air-fryer basket by folding 1 long sheet of aluminum foil so it is 4 inches wide. Lay sheet of foil widthwise across basket, pressing foil into and up sides of basket. Fold excess foil as needed so that edges of foil are flush with top of basket. Lightly spray foil and basket with vegetable oil spray.

2 Combine marmalade, orange zest and juice, and mustard in bowl. Pat salmon dry with paper towels and season with salt and pepper. Brush tops and sides of fillets evenly with glaze. Arrange fillets skin side down on sling in prepared basket, spaced evenly apart. Place basket in air fryer and set temperature to 400 degrees. Cook salmon until center is still translucent when checked with tip of paring knife and registers 125 degrees (for medium-rare), 10 to 14 minutes, using sling to rotate fillets halfway through cooking.

3 Using sling, carefully remove salmon from air fryer. Slide fish spatula along underside of fillets and transfer to individual serving plates, leaving skin behind. Serve.

HONEY-CHIPOTLE GLAZED SALMON
Omit orange zest and juice. Substitute 2 tablespoons honey for marmalade and 2 teaspoons minced canned chipotle chile in adobo sauce for mustard.

HOISIN GLAZED SALMON
Omit orange zest. Substitute 2 tablespoons hoisin sauce for marmalade, 1 tablespoon rice vinegar for orange juice, and ⅛ teaspoon ground ginger for mustard.

SALMON TACOS WITH ROASTED PINEAPPLE SLAW

Serves 2 to 4

COOK TIME 18 minutes   **TOTAL TIME** 50 minutes

why this recipe works California-style fish tacos generally feature deep-fried fish, a tangy cabbage slaw, and a creamy sauce that binds everything together. For a lighter take on this treat, we swapped in salmon for the typical white fish. Since salmon is naturally rich, it wouldn't need to be battered and fried; a spice rub instead gave the fillets a nice crust, and air-frying them skin-on atop a foil sling ensured they would hold together and emerge perfectly moist inside. For a slaw that stood up to the salmon, we wanted to incorporate a bright, fruity element. Pineapple caught our attention; we could roast pieces in the air fryer, allowing them to caramelize a bit before combining them with crunchy coleslaw mix, cilantro, and lime—a perfect bright complement to the fish. For a creamy topping, in lieu of a heavy sour cream–based sauce we mashed avocado with lime juice, salt, and pepper. Spread onto warmed corn tortillas, the avocado mash held the moist, flaky fish and tangy slaw in place for a perfect bite. If using wild salmon, cook it until it registers 120 degrees. For more information on making a foil sling, see page 11.

3 cups (8 ounces) shredded coleslaw mix

¼ cup lime juice (2 limes), plus lime wedges for serving

Salt and pepper

1½ cups ½-inch pineapple pieces

2 teaspoons vegetable oil

1 teaspoon smoked paprika

¼ teaspoon ground coriander

⅛ teaspoon cayenne pepper

2 (8-ounce) skin-on salmon fillets, 1½ inches thick

1 avocado, halved and pitted

2 tablespoons minced fresh cilantro

6-12 (6-inch) corn tortillas, warmed

1 Toss coleslaw mix with 3 tablespoons lime juice, ¼ teaspoon salt, and ⅛ teaspoon pepper in bowl; set aside.

2 Toss pineapple with 1 teaspoon oil in separate bowl; transfer to air-fryer basket. Place basket in air fryer and set temperature to 400 degrees. Cook until pineapple is browned at edges, 12 to 16 minutes, tossing halfway through cooking. Transfer to now-empty bowl and set aside; let air-fryer basket cool slightly.

3 Make foil sling for air-fryer basket by folding 1 long sheet of aluminum foil so it is 4 inches wide. Lay sheet of foil widthwise across basket, pressing foil into and up sides of basket. Fold excess foil as needed so that edges of foil are flush with top of basket. Lightly spray foil and basket with vegetable oil spray.

4 Combine paprika, coriander, cayenne, ⅛ teaspoon salt, and ⅛ teaspoon pepper in small bowl. Pat salmon dry with paper towels, rub with remaining 1 teaspoon oil, and sprinkle tops and sides of fillets with spice mixture. Arrange fillets skin side down on sling in prepared basket, spaced evenly apart. Return basket to air fryer and cook salmon until center is still translucent when checked with tip of paring knife and registers 125 degrees (for medium-rare), 6 to 10 minutes, using sling to rotate fillets halfway through cooking.

5 Meanwhile, using fork, mash avocado with remaining 1 tablespoon lime juice in medium bowl. Season with salt and pepper to taste. Drain coleslaw mixture and return to now-empty bowl. Stir in pineapple and cilantro.

6 Using sling, carefully remove salmon from air fryer. Slide fish spatula along underside of fillets and transfer to plate, leaving skin behind. Using 2 forks, flake salmon into rough 1-inch pieces. Serve on tortillas with slaw and mashed avocado, passing lime wedges separately.

SWORDFISH SKEWERS WITH TOMATO-SCALLION CAPONATA

Serves 2

COOK TIME 20 minutes   **TOTAL TIME** 45 minutes

why this recipe works This simple way to prepare swordfish highlights its distinct taste and texture against a backdrop of robust Mediterranean flavors. Skewered chunks of fish cooked evenly in the air fryer and were easy to serve. For a streamlined caponata, the Sicilian sweet-sour eggplant relish, the air fryer's circulated hot air did a beautiful job of softening and browning mellow eggplant and bright scallions, and of roasting cherry tomatoes until they burst, creating a sauce that helped bind the vegetables, which we coarsely chopped and tossed with warm spices and basil. You can substitute halibut for the swordfish.

- 1 small Italian eggplant (10 ounces), cut into 1-inch pieces
- 6 ounces cherry tomatoes
- 3 scallions, cut into 2-inch lengths
- 2 tablespoons extra-virgin olive oil
- Salt and pepper

- 12 ounces skinless swordfish steaks, 1 ¼ inches thick, cut into 1-inch pieces
- 2 teaspoons honey
- 2 teaspoons ground coriander
- 1 teaspoon grated lemon zest plus 1 teaspoon juice

- 4 (6-inch) wooden skewers
- 1 garlic clove, minced
- ½ teaspoon ground cumin
- 1 tablespoon chopped fresh basil

1 Toss eggplant, tomatoes, and scallions with 1 tablespoon oil, ¼ teaspoon salt, and ⅛ teaspoon pepper in bowl; transfer to air-fryer basket. Place basket in air fryer and set temperature to 400 degrees. Cook until eggplant is softened and browned and tomatoes have begun to burst, about 14 minutes, tossing halfway through cooking. Transfer vegetables to cutting board and set aside to cool slightly.

2 Pat swordfish dry with paper towels. Combine 1 teaspoon oil, 1 teaspoon honey, 1 teaspoon coriander, ½ teaspoon lemon zest, ⅛ teaspoon salt, and pinch pepper in clean bowl. Add swordfish and toss to coat. Thread swordfish onto skewers, leaving about ¼ inch between each piece (3 or 4 pieces per skewer).

3 Arrange skewers in now-empty air-fryer basket, spaced evenly apart. (Skewers may overlap slightly.) Return basket to air fryer and cook until swordfish is browned and registers 140 degrees, 6 to 8 minutes, flipping and rotating skewers halfway through cooking.

4 Meanwhile, combine remaining 2 teaspoons oil, remaining 1 teaspoon honey, remaining 1 teaspoon coriander, remaining ½ teaspoon lemon zest, lemon juice, garlic, cumin, ¼ teaspoon salt, and ⅛ teaspoon pepper in large bowl. Microwave, stirring once, until fragrant, about 30 seconds. Coarsely chop vegetables, transfer to bowl with dressing, along with any accumulated juices, and gently toss to combine. Stir in basil and season with salt and pepper to taste. Serve skewers with caponata.

CRAB CAKES WITH BIBB LETTUCE AND APPLE SALAD

Serves 2

COOK TIME 13 minutes   **TOTAL TIME** 45 minutes

why this recipe works Looking for an elegant meal or appetizer you can assemble with little effort? Make crab cakes in the air fryer; they come out well and there's no messy pan frying. Any good crab cake starts with lots of sweet, plump crabmeat and minimal binder. After blotting away excess moisture, we found 2 tablespoons of panko and an egg were all ours needed. Mayonnaise, Dijon mustard, and cayenne added richness, tang, and gentle heat, and minced scallion contributed subtle aromatics. While the cakes chilled, we air-fried some crispy shallots to garnish a fresh green Bibb and apple salad, which we served with our crab cakes. Buy crabmeat (fresh or pasteurized) packed in plastic containers in the refrigerated section of your fish department. We do not recommend canned crabmeat.

8 ounces lump crabmeat, picked over for shells	1½ teaspoons Dijon mustard	⅛ teaspoon salt
	Pinch cayenne pepper	Pinch pepper
2 tablespoons panko bread crumbs	2 shallots, sliced thin	½ small head Bibb lettuce (3 ounces), torn into bite-size pieces
1 scallion, minced	1 tablespoon extra-virgin olive oil	
1 large egg		½ apple, cored and sliced thin
1 tablespoon mayonnaise	1 teaspoon lemon juice, plus lemon wedges for serving	

1 Line large plate with triple layer of paper towels. Transfer crabmeat to prepared plate and pat dry with additional paper towels. Combine panko, scallion, egg, mayonnaise, mustard, and cayenne in bowl. Using rubber spatula, gently fold in crabmeat until combined; discard paper towels. Divide crab mixture into 4 tightly packed balls, then flatten each into 1-inch-thick cake (cakes will be delicate). Transfer cakes to now-empty plate and refrigerate until firm, about 10 minutes.

2 Toss shallots with ½ teaspoon oil in separate bowl; transfer to air-fryer basket. Place basket in air fryer and set temperature to 400 degrees. Cook until shallots are browned, 5 to 7 minutes, tossing once halfway through cooking. Return shallots to now-empty bowl and set aside.

3 Arrange crab cakes in now-empty air-fryer basket, spaced evenly apart. Return basket to air fryer and cook until crab cakes are light golden brown on both sides, 8 to 10 minutes, flipping and rotating cakes halfway through cooking.

4 Meanwhile, whisk remaining 2½ teaspoons oil, lemon juice, salt, and pepper together in large bowl. Add lettuce, apple, and shallots and toss to coat. Serve crab cakes with salad, passing lemon wedges separately.

THAI SHRIMP SKEWERS WITH PEANUT DIPPING SAUCE

Serves 2

COOK TIME 6 minutes   **TOTAL TIME** 50 minutes

why this recipe works Shrimp cook very quickly—that's one reason we love them—and they can turn from moist and juicy to rubbery and dry in the blink of an eye. For juicy, boldly seasoned shrimp in the air fryer, we employed a time-honored test kitchen technique: brining. Just 15 minutes in a salty brine helped the shelled and deveined shrimp hang on to their moisture during cooking, and the brine seasoned them evenly throughout. Next, inspired by Thai street food, we coated the brined shrimp in a potent paste of oil, honey, and lime zest and threaded them onto skewers for easy maneuvering in the air fryer and an attractive presentation. After just 6 minutes, they emerged plump, juicy, and deeply flavored, and with a burnished sheen. We then whipped up a simple but classic peanut dipping sauce to serve with our Thai-style shrimp skewers. We whisked together creamy peanut butter, lime juice, cilantro, and a touch of pungent fish sauce, thinning out the sauce with hot water. Dipped in this sauce, our shrimp skewers offered a perfect balance of sweet, salty, and vibrant flavors. Serve with rice or steamed vegetables.

Salt and pepper

12 ounces extra-large shrimp (21 to 25 per pound), peeled and deveined

1 tablespoon vegetable oil

1 teaspoon honey

½ teaspoon grated lime zest plus 1 tablespoon juice, plus lime wedges for serving

6 (6-inch) wooden skewers

3 tablespoons creamy peanut butter

3 tablespoons hot tap water

1 tablespoon chopped fresh cilantro

1 teaspoon fish sauce

1 Dissolve 2 tablespoons salt in 1 quart cold water in large container. Add shrimp, cover, and refrigerate for 15 minutes.

2 Remove shrimp from brine and pat dry with paper towels. Whisk oil, honey, lime zest, and ¼ teaspoon pepper together in large bowl. Add shrimp and toss to coat. Thread shrimp onto skewers, leaving about ¼ inch between each shrimp (3 or 4 shrimp per skewer).

3 Arrange 3 skewers in air-fryer basket, parallel to each other and spaced evenly apart. Arrange remaining 3 skewers on top, perpendicular to bottom layer. Place basket in air fryer and set temperature to 400 degrees. Cook until shrimp are opaque throughout, 6 to 8 minutes, flipping and rotating skewers halfway through cooking.

4 Whisk peanut butter, hot tap water, lime juice, cilantro, and fish sauce together in bowl until smooth. Serve skewers with peanut dipping sauce and lime wedges.

BACON-WRAPPED SCALLOPS WITH SPINACH, FENNEL, AND RASPBERRY SALAD

Serves 4

COOK TIME 12 minutes   **TOTAL TIME** 50 minutes

why this recipe works Smoky bacon beautifully accents sweet, briny scallops. The pair are often grilled, but the air fryer offered a foolproof, unfussy way to enjoy this combo without risk of sticking. Since scallops cook much faster than bacon, we parcooked bacon strips in the microwave before wrapping each strip around two scallops (for an ideal scallop-to-bacon ratio) and skewering them. Served with a bright, crunchy spinach salad with fennel and juicy berries, this is an easy and elegant dinner for four. We recommend buying "dry" scallops, which don't have chemical additives and taste better than "wet." Dry scallops will look ivory or pinkish; wet scallops are bright white. Do not use thick-cut bacon.

12 slices bacon

24 large sea scallops, tendons removed

1 teaspoon plus 2 tablespoons extra-virgin olive oil

Salt and pepper

6 (6-inch) wooden skewers

1 tablespoon cider vinegar

1 teaspoon Dijon mustard

5 ounces (5 cups) baby spinach

1 fennel bulb, stalks discarded, bulb halved, cored, and sliced thin

5 ounces (1 cup) raspberries

1 Line large plate with 4 layers paper towels and arrange 6 slices bacon over towels in single layer. Top with 4 more layers paper towels and remaining 6 slices bacon. Cover with 2 layers of paper towels, place second large plate on top, and press gently to flatten. Microwave until fat begins to render but bacon is still pliable, about 5 minutes.

2 Pat scallops dry with paper towels and toss with 1 teaspoon oil, ⅛ teaspoon salt, and ⅛ teaspoon pepper in bowl until evenly coated. Arrange 2 scallops side to side, flat side down, on cutting board. Starting at narrow end, wrap 1 slice bacon tightly around sides of scallop bundle. (Bacon should overlap slightly; trim excess as needed.) Thread scallop bundle onto skewer through bacon. Repeat with remaining scallops and bacon, threading 2 bundles onto each skewer.

3 Arrange 3 skewers in air-fryer basket, parallel to each other and spaced evenly apart. Arrange remaining 3 skewers on top, perpendicular to bottom layer. Place basket in air fryer and set temperature to 350 degrees. Cook until bacon is crisp and scallops are firm and centers are opaque, 12 to 16 minutes, flipping and rotating skewers halfway through cooking.

4 Meanwhile, whisk remaining 2 tablespoons oil, vinegar, mustard, ⅛ teaspoon salt, and ⅛ teaspoon pepper in large serving bowl until combined. Add spinach, fennel, and raspberries and gently toss to coat. Serve skewers with salad.

SOUTH CAROLINA—STYLE SHRIMP BAKE

Serves 2

COOK TIME 18 minutes   **TOTAL TIME** 30 minutes

why this recipe works South Carolina's seafood boil features shell-on shrimp, smoked sausage, corn on the cob, and potatoes simmered in an Old Bay–spiked broth. Translating a stew meant for large gatherings to the air fryer might sound curious, but we had a hunch that it would prove ideal for two people, speeding up the process (no need to boil water!) and concentrating the flavors in the hot-air environment. Just like the boiled original, the dish would be a one-"pot" meal, which is a big part of its charm but can also be its downfall. Cooks often throw everything into the pot at once, resulting in mushy potatoes, mealy corn, and rubbery shrimp. The same proved true in the air fryer. We found that staggering the cooking times of the components permitted each to cook just right. We started by seasoning cubes of potatoes and 2-inch rounds of corn with Old Bay and giving them a head start in the air fryer. Meanwhile, we tossed andouille sausage and shrimp (with the shells snipped for easy peeling but left on to protect the delicate meat) with more Old Bay and a liberal dose of minced garlic. Adding them to the basket on top of the vegetables brought them close to the heating element for better browning; they cooked through in almost no time. In just 30 minutes we were able to produce tender potatoes and corn, juicy shrimp, and smoky sausage, perhaps the easiest-ever take on the South Carolina classic.

8 ounces red potatoes, unpeeled, cut into 1-inch pieces

1 ear corn, husk and silk removed, cut into 2-inch rounds

2 teaspoons vegetable oil

2 teaspoons Old Bay seasoning

¼ teaspoon pepper

8 ounces extra-large shrimp (21 to 25 per pound)

6 ounces andouille or chorizo sausage, cut into 1-inch pieces

2 garlic cloves, minced

1 tablespoon chopped fresh parsley

1 Toss potatoes and corn with 1 teaspoon oil, 1 teaspoon Old Bay, and pepper in bowl; transfer to air-fryer basket. Place basket in air fryer, set temperature to 400 degrees, and cook for 12 minutes, tossing halfway through cooking.

2 Using kitchen shears or sharp paring knife, cut through shell of shrimp and devein but do not remove shell. Using paring knife, continue to cut shrimp ½ inch deep, taking care not to cut in half completely.

3 Toss shrimp and sausage with garlic, remaining 1 teaspoon oil, and remaining 1 teaspoon Old Bay in now-empty bowl. Arrange shrimp and sausage on top of vegetables. Return basket to air fryer and cook until shrimp are opaque throughout, 6 to 8 minutes, tossing halfway through cooking. Transfer to serving platter and sprinkle with parsley. Serve.

VEGETABLES

ROASTED ASPARAGUS

Serves 4

COOK TIME 6 minutes   **TOTAL TIME** 15 minutes

why this recipe works There are many reasons to cook vegetables in your air fryer, and not just fried renditions of them. The air fryer's convection heat ably cooks vegetables of all kinds—without hogging valuable oven space. While we loved using it to roast sturdy root vegetables, perhaps its simplest application was to cook a bunch of asparagus. Because of asparagus' high water content, we found it best to avoid taking the spears to the point of crispness, which dried them out. Instead, we let the air fryer's circulated heat cook the asparagus until vibrant green and crisp-tender, akin to what we might produce through boiling but without the risk of a waterlogged, mushy outcome. The asparagus needed just a teaspoon of oil and in 6 minutes they emerged perfectly cooked. We love asparagus served simply with lemon wedges, but for more bright flavor, pair it with a gremolata topping.

1 pound asparagus, trimmed and halved crosswise

1 teaspoon extra-virgin olive oil

Salt and pepper

Lemon wedges

Toss asparagus with oil, ⅛ teaspoon salt, and ⅛ teaspoon pepper in bowl; transfer to air-fryer basket. Place basket in air fryer and set temperature to 400 degrees. Cook asparagus until tender and bright green, 6 to 8 minutes, tossing halfway through cooking. Season with salt and pepper to taste. Serve with lemon wedges.

MINT-ORANGE GREMOLATA
Combine 2 tablespoons minced fresh mint, 2 tablespoons minced fresh parsley, 2 teaspoons grated orange zest, 1 minced garlic clove, and pinch cayenne pepper in bowl.

TARRAGON-LEMON GREMOLATA
Combine 2 tablespoons minced fresh tarragon, 2 tablespoons minced fresh parsley, 2 teaspoons grated lemon zest, and 1 minced garlic clove in bowl.

AIR-FRIED BRUSSELS SPROUTS

Serves 4

COOK TIME 20 minutes   **TOTAL TIME** 25 minutes

why this recipe works Fried Brussels sprouts have become a menu staple—and for good reason. The tiny cabbages caramelize and crisp while maintaining enough structure to work as a dipping vessel. Of course, deep-frying them is something of a project and doesn't yield the healthiest results. We wanted to see if we could use the air fryer to make "fried" Brussels sprouts that kept their virtuous qualities but tasted as decadent as their deep-fried counterparts. Our first attempts were promising but not perfect. Since we usually achieve crispiness (when not frying) by using a very hot oven, we tossed the Brussels sprouts in a little oil and roasted them in the air fryer at 400 degrees. They crisped up but tasted raw inside: The air fryer was doing too good a job at browning. We tried adding a splash of water before cooking the sprouts, hoping the resulting steam might soften them faster, but no luck. The solution turned out to be more obvious: Lowering the heat to 350 gave the sprouts time to soften on the inside while crisping. The results mimicked the deep-fried sprouts so well that we were inspired to create a version with another beloved fried vegetable: crispy shallots. Both versions were delicious with a squeeze of lemon, but irresistible with Lemon-Chive Dipping Sauce. If you are buying loose Brussels sprouts, select those that are about 1½ inches long. Quarter Brussels sprouts longer than 2½ inches.

1 pound Brussels sprouts, trimmed and halved

1 tablespoon extra-virgin olive oil

Salt and pepper

Lemon wedges

Toss Brussels sprouts with oil, ¼ teaspoon salt, and ⅛ teaspoon pepper in bowl; transfer to air-fryer basket. Place basket in air fryer and set temperature 350 degrees. Cook Brussels sprouts until tender, well browned, and crisp, 20 to 25 minutes, tossing halfway through cooking. Season with salt and pepper to taste. Serve with lemon wedges.

AIR-FRIED BRUSSELS SPROUTS WITH CRISPY SHALLOTS
Add 3 thinly sliced shallots to bowl with Brussels sprouts along with oil, salt, and pepper.

LEMON-CHIVE DIPPING SAUCE
Whisk together ¼ cup mayonnaise, 1 tablespoon minced fresh chives, ½ teaspoon grated lemon zest plus 2 teaspoons juice, ½ teaspoon Worcestershire sauce, ½ teaspoon Dijon mustard, and ¼ teaspoon garlic powder in bowl.

ORANGE-CARDAMOM ROASTED CARROTS

Serves 4

COOK TIME 30 minutes   **TOTAL TIME** 45 minutes

why this recipe works Crunchy and fairly bland when raw, carrots become sweet and buttery when roasted, with chewy caramelized edges. We had those edges in mind when we set out to roast carrots in the air fryer, initially cutting them into coins to create plenty of surface area that we hoped would produce maximum browning. Disappointingly, the carrots came out shriveled. Such small pieces were no match for the intense hot air. We realized we needed bigger pieces, which would have more time to brown before overcooking. Indeed, this improved the carrots' texture, but we still wanted more browning and found our solution in the coating: Switching from oil to butter (which contains milk solids that brown quickly) and adding honey (which caramelizes quickly) gave us deep roasted color and flavor. For even more flavor, we bloomed cardamom and orange zest in the butter as it melted, reserving a portion for a satiny glaze—adding a splash of juice for acidity. Now we had beautifully roasted carrots draped in an addictive glaze; with just a sprinkle of fresh chives, this side dish was complete. If the carrots have very narrow tips, trim the thin ends; they scorch easily.

- 2 tablespoons unsalted butter
- 1 tablespoon honey
- ½ teaspoon grated orange zest plus 1 tablespoon juice

- ½ teaspoon ground cardamom
- Salt and pepper

- 2 pounds carrots, peeled and cut into 2-inch lengths, thick ends halved lengthwise
- 1 tablespoon minced fresh chives

1 Microwave butter, honey, orange zest, cardamom, and ¼ teaspoon salt in large bowl at 50 percent power, stirring occasionally, until butter is melted, about 1 minute. Whisk to combine. Combine 1 tablespoon butter mixture and orange juice in small bowl; set aside. Add carrots to remaining butter mixture and toss to coat; transfer to air-fryer basket.

2 Place basket in air fryer and set temperature to 400 degrees. Cook carrots until tender and browned, about 30 minutes, tossing every 10 minutes.

3 Transfer carrots to now-empty bowl and toss with reserved butter mixture. Season with salt and pepper to taste and sprinkle with chives. Serve.

CUMIN-LIME ROASTED CARROTS
Substitute lime zest for orange zest, 1 teaspoon lime juice for orange juice, cumin for cardamom, and cilantro for chives.

SMOKED PAPRIKA—LEMON ROASTED CARROTS
Substitute lemon zest for orange zest, 1 teaspoon lemon juice for orange juice, smoked paprika for cardamom, and mint for chives.

CURRIED ROASTED CAULIFLOWER AND CHICKPEA SALAD

Serves 4

| COOK TIME 23 minutes | TOTAL TIME 45 minutes |

why this recipe works Roasting brings out the best in cauliflower, giving the otherwise plain vegetable a nutty sweetness. Given our love of roasted cauliflower, we were excited to discover that we could roast an entire head's worth of florets in the air fryer at once, and in less time than it takes in an oven. We just had to ensure the pieces cooked evenly, which was easily achieved by tossing the florets halfway through cooking to redistribute them. A bit of curry powder and olive oil tossed on the florets before roasting enhanced their golden hue. While the cauliflower cooked and cooled, we assembled other components to turn it into a flavorful salad: a tangy cilantro-lime yogurt dressing, chickpeas for substance, red grapes for sweetness, and chopped cashews for crunch. We mixed everything up, and with an extra sprinkle of cilantro our roasted cauliflower salad was done, easy enough to be a simple side or a light lunch any day.

3½ tablespoons extra-virgin olive oil

1½ teaspoons curry powder

Salt and pepper

1 head cauliflower (2 pounds), cored and cut into 1½-inch florets

¼ cup plain yogurt

2 tablespoons chopped fresh cilantro

1½ teaspoons lime juice

1 garlic clove, minced

1 (15-ounce) can chickpeas, rinsed

3 ounces seedless red grapes, halved (½ cup)

¼ cup roasted cashews, chopped

1 Whisk 1½ tablespoons oil, curry powder, ⅛ teaspoon salt, and ⅛ teaspoon pepper together in medium bowl. Add cauliflower and toss to coat; transfer to air-fryer basket. Place basket in air fryer and set temperature to 400 degrees. Cook cauliflower until tender and golden at edges, 23 to 25 minutes, tossing halfway through cooking.

2 Set cauliflower aside to cool slightly. Meanwhile, whisk yogurt, 1 tablespoon cilantro, lime juice, garlic, ⅛ teaspoon salt, ⅛ teaspoon pepper, and remaining 2 tablespoons oil together in serving bowl. Add cooled cauliflower and chickpeas and toss to coat. Season with salt and pepper to taste. Sprinkle with grapes, cashews, and remaining 1 tablespoon cilantro. Serve.

ROASTED GREEN BEANS WITH SUN-DRIED TOMATOES AND SUNFLOWER SEEDS

Serves 4

COOK TIME 12 minutes

TOTAL TIME 30 minutes

why this recipe works There may be no sadder side dish than the pile of army-green, bland, spoon-soft green beans many of us recall from childhood. On the flip side, green beans can be the most vibrant of vegetables and a wonderful base for a salad bursting with flavors, textures, and colors. The air fryer made the job easy: Just 12 minutes at a high temperature gave us bright, crisp-tender green beans that retained all of their grassy, sweet flavor. Now we had to do them justice with additions. Umami-rich sun-dried tomatoes and fresh basil gave the salad contrasting flavors: briny, sweet, and herbal. Goat cheese added creamy richness. In lieu of the almonds often paired with green beans, we turned to earthy sunflower seeds to finish the dish with a nutty crunch. Lemon juice brought clean acidity, and olive oil rounded out the punch for a simple dressing. With little work we had a green bean salad overflowing with flavors and redolent of a summer garden, a perfect match for all kinds of main dishes. You can use the air fryer to roast sunflower seeds; see page 13.

- 1 pound green beans, trimmed and halved
- 2 teaspoons extra-virgin olive oil
- Salt and pepper

- ½ cup torn fresh basil
- ⅓ cup oil-packed sun-dried tomatoes, rinsed, patted dry, and chopped

- 1 tablespoon lemon juice
- 2 ounces goat cheese, crumbled (½ cup)
- ¼ cup roasted sunflower seeds

1 Toss green beans with 1 teaspoon oil, ⅛ teaspoon salt, and ⅛ teaspoon pepper in bowl; transfer to air-fryer basket. Place basket in air fryer and set temperature to 400 degrees. Cook green beans until crisp-tender, 12 to 15 minutes, tossing halfway through cooking.

2 Toss green beans with remaining 1 teaspoon oil, basil, sun-dried tomatoes, and lemon juice in large bowl. Season with salt and pepper to taste. Transfer to serving dish and sprinkle with goat cheese and sunflower seeds. Serve.

ROASTED BELL PEPPER SALAD WITH MOZZARELLA AND BASIL

Serves 2

COOK TIME 25 minutes   **TOTAL TIME** 1 hour

why this recipe works Roasting bell peppers on the grill or over a direct flame can be a pain: Unevenly charred, black skin sticks to everything and can be frustrating to peel off. But jarred roasted peppers, despite their convenience, don't have the same fresh flavor or meaty texture. So we were thrilled to find that the air fryer does a beautiful job of roasting bell peppers. Twenty-five minutes after tucking four small bell peppers snugly on their sides in the air-fryer basket, we had well-browned, wrinkled skin and tender flesh. After a quick steam, the skin peeled off cleanly. To showcase our sweet, meaty roasted peppers, we paired them with a balsamic dressing, creamy fresh mozzarella, fragrant basil, and toasted pine nuts for a deeply flavored salad. Choose a mix of red, yellow, and orange bell peppers for the most attractive presentation. Be sure to buy peppers that will fit comfortably on their sides in your air fryer. You can use your air fryer to toast pine nuts; see page 13.

4 small bell peppers (red, orange, and/or yellow)

2 tablespoons extra-virgin olive oil

1 tablespoon balsamic vinegar

1 garlic clove, minced

Salt and pepper

2 ounces fresh mozzarella cheese, torn into 1-inch pieces

2 tablespoons torn fresh basil

1 tablespoon pine nuts, toasted

1 Trim ½ inch from top and bottom of bell peppers. Using paring knife, remove ribs, core, and seeds and discard. Arrange bell peppers in air-fryer basket on their sides. (Bell peppers will fit snugly.) Place basket in air fryer and set temperature to 400 degrees. Cook bell peppers until skins are brown and wrinkled and have collapsed, about 25 minutes, flipping and rotating bell peppers halfway through cooking. Transfer bell peppers to bowl, cover tightly with plastic wrap, and let steam for 10 minutes.

2 Whisk oil, vinegar, garlic, ⅛ teaspoon salt, and ⅛ teaspoon pepper together in serving dish. Uncover bowl to let bell peppers cool slightly. When cool enough to handle, peel bell peppers and discard skin, then cut bell peppers into 1-inch-wide strips. Add bell peppers and mozzarella to bowl with dressing and toss to coat; season with salt and pepper to taste. Sprinkle with basil and pine nuts. Serve.

ROASTED BELL PEPPER SALAD WITH MANCHEGO AND OLIVES

Substitute sherry vinegar for balsamic vinegar and add 2 teaspoons minced fresh marjoram (or oregano) to dressing in step 2. Substitute 1 ounce shaved Manchego for mozzarella. Substitute ¼ cup sliced pitted green olives for basil. Substitute 2 tablespoons toasted slivered almonds for pine nuts.

BAKED POTATOES

Serves 2

COOK TIME 40 minutes   **TOTAL TIME** 55 minutes

why this recipe works One great advantage of an air fryer is how it untethers you from your oven—no more heating up the house for a small project. Enter baked potatoes: Typically requiring at least an hour of oven time at high heat, simple baked potatoes can become a nuisance on a hot day, or when trying to bake another dish at a different temperature. The air fryer handily solved that problem. With no need to preheat, it took just 40 minutes to bake two fluffy, tender potatoes. Our foolproof method of lightly oiling and salting the outside of the potatoes produced crisp, tasty, well-seasoned skins, and poking holes for steam to escape ensured the centers became fluffy. Top the potatoes as desired or with one of our compound butters.

2 russet potatoes   ¼ teaspoon   Salt and pepper
   (8 ounces each),   vegetable oil
   unpeeled

1 Lightly prick each potato several times with fork. Rub potatoes with oil and sprinkle with ⅛ teaspoon salt. Arrange potatoes in air-fryer basket, spaced evenly apart. Place basket in air fryer and set temperature to 400 degrees. Cook until paring knife inserted into potatoes meets little resistance, 40 to 45 minutes.

2 Transfer potatoes to large plate and, using paring knife, cut 2 slits, forming X, in each potato. Press in at ends of potatoes to push flesh up and out. Season with salt and pepper to taste. Serve.

BLUE CHEESE–PEPPER BUTTER
Mash 1½ tablespoons softened unsalted butter, 1 tablespoon crumbled blue cheese, and ¼ teaspoon pepper together in bowl.

LEMON-THYME BUTTER
Mash 2 tablespoons softened unsalted butter, 1 teaspoon minced fresh thyme, and ¼ teaspoon grated lemon zest and ¼ teaspoon juice together in bowl.

CRISPY SMASHED POTATOES

Serves 2 to 4

COOK TIME 40 minutes   **TOTAL TIME** 1 hour

why this recipe works Smashed potatoes offer the best of both worlds: the crackling crust of roast potatoes and a creamy mashed potato–like interior. Traditionally, the potatoes are boiled and then flattened and crisped in a hot pan of oil. However, the air fryer crisped the smashed potatoes even more thoroughly, as the hot air made its way into the broken potatoes' many cracks and crevices to produce an intensely crackly exterior (the air fryer also required less oil). Better still, we could skip the boiling and steam the potatoes in a foil packet in the air fryer, which not only simplified the process but intensified the potatoes' earthy flavor. We chose red potatoes for their moist texture and thin skin. After steaming them until soft, we used a baking sheet to press on all of the potatoes at once, cracking and flattening them to ½ inch. (A potato masher can also be used.) After tossing them with olive oil, salt, pepper, and fresh thyme, we returned them to the air fryer, where they crisped to perfection. We found that not stirring or shaking the basket during the final 15 minutes helped produce an even more pronounced crunchy outer layer. Use small red potatoes measuring no larger than 1½ inches in diameter.

1½ pounds small red
     potatoes, unpeeled

2 tablespoons extra-
   virgin olive oil

1 teaspoon chopped
   fresh thyme

   Salt and pepper

1 Arrange potatoes in center of large sheet of aluminum foil and lift sides to form bowl. Pour ¾ cup water over potatoes and crimp foil tightly to seal. Place foil packet in air-fryer basket, place basket in air fryer, and set temperature to 400 degrees. Cook until paring knife inserted into potatoes meets little resistance (poke through foil to test), 25 to 30 minutes.

2 Carefully open foil packet, allowing steam to escape away from you, and let cool slightly. Arrange potatoes in single layer on cutting board; discard foil. Place baking sheet on top of potatoes and press down firmly on baking sheet, flattening potatoes to ½-inch thickness.

Transfer smashed potatoes to large bowl; drizzle with oil and sprinkle with thyme, ½ teaspoon salt, and ⅛ teaspoon pepper. Toss until well combined and most potatoes have broken apart into chunks.

3 Return potatoes to air fryer and cook until well browned and crispy (do not stir or shake during cooking), 15 to 20 minutes. Season with salt and pepper to taste. Serve.

CRISPY SMASHED POTATOES WITH GARLIC AND DILL

Substitute chopped fresh dill for thyme. Add ½ teaspoon garlic powder to potatoes with oil in step 2.

CHEESY POTATOES

Serves 2

COOK TIME 32 minutes   **TOTAL TIME** 1 hour

why this recipe works When it came to the best ingredients to air-fry, potatoes were naturals: From roasted fingerlings to smashed baby Bliss and French-fried russets, the air fryer made delicious work of all of them. This made us think more ambitiously: Could we bake a bubbly cheese and potato gratin in the perforated basket? We weren't keen on using extra equipment such as a mini casserole. Fortunately, a foil sling worked fine and enabled us to shape it just large enough to hold our ingredients while allowing space for the air circulation that makes the air fryer so effective. After tossing thinly sliced potatoes with butter and seasonings, we shingled them in layers, sprinkling cheese in between. A mix of nutty Parmesan and cheddar gave the best mix of flavor and texture. To prevent the top layer of cheese from burning, we waited to add it until the potatoes were completely tender. The result was a gorgeous, decadent gratin sized just right for two people. Use the large holes of a box grater to shred the cheddar and Parmesan cheese.

2 ounces cheddar cheese, shredded (½ cup)

¼ cup shredded Parmesan cheese

1 tablespoon unsalted butter

1 garlic clove, minced

1 teaspoon minced fresh thyme or ¼ teaspoon dried

Salt and pepper

1 pound russet potatoes, unpeeled, sliced ¼ inch thick

1 Make foil sling for air-fryer basket by folding 1 long sheet of aluminum foil so it is 4 inches wide. Lay sheet of foil widthwise across basket, pressing foil into and up sides of basket. Fold excess foil as needed so that edges of foil are flush with top of basket. Lightly spray foil and basket with vegetable oil spray.

2 Combine cheddar and Parmesan in bowl; set aside. Microwave butter, garlic, thyme, ¼ teaspoon salt, and ⅛ teaspoon pepper in large bowl at 50 percent power, stirring occasionally, until butter is melted, about 1 minute. Add potatoes and toss to coat. Shingle half of potatoes in single layer in prepared basket, covering center of foil. Sprinkle potatoes with half of cheese mixture. Shingle remaining potatoes in single layer over top.

3 Place basket in air fryer and set temperature to 400 degrees. Cook potatoes until tender and crispy at edges, 30 to 35 minutes, using sling to rotate potatoes halfway through cooking. Sprinkle potatoes with remaining cheese mixture. Return basket to air fryer and cook until cheese is bubbly and golden brown, about 2 minutes.

4 Using foil sling, carefully remove potatoes from basket and transfer to serving dish. Season with salt and pepper to taste. Serve.

FRENCH FRIES

Serves 2 to 4

COOK TIME 28 minutes   **TOTAL TIME** 1 hour

why this recipe works After years of turning out fries of every stripe, we know a good fry when we taste one: the browned, crisp exterior, the fluffy center. And we know that achieving this ideal requires a few tricks, typically a presoak and a two-part frying. But who can argue with the promise of fries cooked with minimal effort or oil? So, holding doubts in check, we set out to create the ideal air-fryer French fry. Some recipes called for hours of prework. Others had you throw the potatoes in the basket and cross your fingers. From dry, hollow sticks to limp, greasy planks, not one passed muster. Seventy pounds of potatoes later, we learned that air-fryer fries require the same tricks as their deep-fried cousins: soaking, a low-temp fry to par-cook the spuds, and a high-temp fry to crisp them. But we found shortcuts: A rinse and a 10-minute soak in hot water was sufficient. Cutting thick fries prevented hollow centers and yielded a great crispy-fluffy ratio. Still, our fries tasted lean. A second toss in a bit of oil and salt in between fryings proved the solution, producing crisp, perfectly seasoned results. Excellent homemade fries had never been easier. Frequently tossing the potatoes ensured the most even cooking and the best browning. We found tossing the fries in a bowl, rather than in the basket, yielded the best results and the fewest broken fries. Do not clean out the tossing bowl while you are cooking; the residual oil helps the crisping process. Serve with Sriracha Dipping Sauce.

1½   **pounds russet   2 tablespoons   Salt and pepper
      potatoes, peeled   vegetable oil**

1 Cut potatoes lengthwise into ½-inch-thick planks. Stack 3 or 4 planks and cut into ½-inch-thick sticks; repeat with remaining planks.

2 Submerge potatoes in large bowl of water and rinse to remove excess starch. Drain potatoes and repeat process as needed until water remains clear. Cover potatoes with hot tap water and let sit for 10 minutes. Drain potatoes, transfer to paper towel–lined rimmed baking sheet, and thoroughly pat dry.

3 Toss potatoes with 1 tablespoon oil in clean, dry bowl, then transfer to air-fryer basket. Place basket in air fryer, set temperature to 350 degrees, and cook for 8 minutes. Transfer potatoes to now-empty bowl and gently toss to redistribute. Return potatoes to air fryer and cook until softened and potatoes have turned from white to blond (potatoes may be spotty brown at tips), 5 to 10 minutes.

4 Transfer potatoes to now-empty bowl and toss with remaining 1 tablespoon oil and ½ teaspoon salt. Return potatoes to air fryer, increase temperature to 400 degrees, and cook until golden brown and crisp, 15 to 20 minutes, tossing gently in bowl to redistribute every 5 minutes. Transfer fries to large plate and season with salt and pepper to taste. Serve immediately.

SRIRACHA DIPPING SAUCE

Whisk ¼ cup mayonnaise, 1 tablespoon sriracha, 1 tablespoon lime juice, 1½ teaspoons grated fresh ginger, and ⅛ teaspoon soy sauce together in bowl.

PARMESAN, ROSEMARY, AND BLACK PEPPER FRENCH FRIES

Serves 2 to 4

COOK TIME 28 minutes   **TOTAL TIME** 1 hour

why this recipe works Once we learned how to make crave-worthy French fries in the air fryer, we thought that giving them a Parmesan-rosemary coating would be a cinch. We tossed the hot fries with grated cheese and minced herbs, but only some adhered; the rest fell to the bottom of the bowl. Switching gears, we added the cheese partway through cooking. Now the cheese clung and even crisped into a coating, but it lost some of its Parmesan flavor. The Goldilocks moment came when we cooked some cheese onto the fries for a crust, then tossed more with the cooked fries for flavor. (Adding the rosemary both during and after cooking also best highlighted the herb's aroma.) To gild the lily, we added a background of black pepper and sprinkled a third handful of cheese onto the finished fry pile, which melted into a lacy coating. Frequently tossing the fries ensured the most even cooking and the best browning. We found tossing the fries in a bowl, rather than in the air-fryer basket, yielded the best results and the fewest broken fries. Do not clean out the tossing bowl while you are cooking; the residual oil helps the crisping process.

1½ **pounds russet potatoes, unpeeled**

2 **tablespoons vegetable oil**

1½ **ounces Parmesan cheese, grated (¾ cup)**

4 **teaspoons minced fresh rosemary**

Salt and pepper

1 Cut potatoes lengthwise into ½-inch-thick planks. Stack 3 or 4 planks and cut into ½-inch-thick sticks; repeat with remaining planks.

2 Submerge potatoes in large bowl of water and rinse to remove excess starch. Drain potatoes and repeat process as needed until water remains clear. Cover potatoes with hot tap water and let sit for 10 minutes. Drain potatoes, transfer to paper towel–lined rimmed baking sheet, and thoroughly pat dry.

3 Toss potatoes with 1 tablespoon oil in clean, dry bowl, then transfer to air-fryer basket. Place basket in air fryer, set temperature to 350 degrees, and cook for 8 minutes. Transfer potatoes to now-empty bowl and gently toss to

redistribute. Return potatoes to air fryer and cook until softened and potatoes have turned from white to blond (potatoes may be spotty brown at tips), 5 to 10 minutes.

4 Transfer potatoes to now-empty bowl and toss with ¼ cup Parmesan, 1 tablespoon rosemary, remaining 1 tablespoon oil, ¼ teaspoon salt, and ¼ teaspoon pepper. Return potatoes to air fryer, increase temperature to 400 degrees, and cook until golden brown and crisp, 15 to 20 minutes, tossing gently in bowl to redistribute every 5 minutes.

5 Transfer fries to bowl and toss with ¼ cup Parmesan and remaining 1 teaspoon rosemary. Season with salt and pepper to taste. Transfer to larger plate and sprinkle with remaining ¼ cup Parmesan. Serve immediately.

BBQ POTATO WEDGES

Serves 2 to 4

COOK TIME 28 minutes　　　　　　　　**TOTAL TIME** 1 hour

why this recipe works The air fryer produces potato wedges with crisp, golden edges and fluffy centers to sink your teeth into. Cutting ½-inch wedges gave us attractively slender spears that fit in the basket and provided plenty of pillowy middle. We avoided using overly long potatoes, which broke during tossing. The cooking method followed in step with our French fries—a quick soak and two-part frying, intermittently tossing the wedges in oil for crispness and flavor. To give our wedges character, we developed several spice blends to toss with the potatoes during their final cook. We found tossing the wedges in a bowl, rather than in the air-fryer basket, yielded the best results and the fewest broken wedges. Do not clean out the tossing bowl while you are cooking; the residual oil helps the crisping process. Use potatoes that are 5 inches long or less; longer potatoes tend to break during tossing.

- 1½　pounds russet potatoes, unpeeled, cut into ½-inch wedges
- 2　tablespoons vegetable oil
- 1　teaspoon chili powder
- 1　teaspoon packed brown sugar
- 　Salt and pepper
- ⅛　teaspoon cayenne pepper

1 Submerge potatoes in large bowl of water and rinse to remove excess starch. Drain potatoes and repeat process as needed until water remains clear. Cover potatoes with hot tap water and let sit for 10 minutes. Drain potatoes, transfer to paper towel–lined rimmed baking sheet, and thoroughly pat dry.

2 Toss potatoes with 1 tablespoon oil in clean, dry bowl, then transfer to air-fryer basket. Place basket in air fryer, set temperature to 350 degrees, and cook for 8 minutes. Transfer potatoes to now-empty bowl and gently toss to redistribute. Return potatoes to air fryer and cook until potatoes are just beginning to soften, 5 to 10 minutes.

3 Transfer potatoes to now-empty bowl and toss with remaining 1 tablespoon oil, chili powder, brown sugar, ½ teaspoon salt, ¼ teaspoon pepper, and cayenne. Return potatoes to air fryer, increase temperature to 400 degrees, and cook until golden brown and crisp, 15 to 20 minutes, tossing gently in bowl to redistribute every 5 minutes. Transfer wedges to large plate and season with salt and pepper to taste. Serve immediately.

LATIN POTATO WEDGES

Omit brown sugar, pepper, and cayenne. Add 1 teaspoon ground cumin, ½ teaspoon ground coriander, and ⅛ teaspoon ground cinnamon to potatoes with oil in step 3.

STEAKHOUSE POTATO WEDGES

Omit chili powder, brown sugar, and cayenne. Increase pepper to 1 teaspoon and add 1 teaspoon ground coriander and ½ teaspoon dried dill to potatoes with oil in step 3.

MAPLE-GLAZED ACORN SQUASH

Serves 2 to 4

COOK TIME 19 minutes   **TOTAL TIME** 35 minutes

why this recipe works Acorn squash and the air fryer are a winning combination: Acorn squash's petite size makes it easy to fit an entire squash inside the basket. To add to its appeal, the squash doesn't need to be peeled—its dark-green skin is edible and provides a visually stunning contrast to its bright orange flesh—and it slices easily into attractive uniform wedges. The squash takes well to roasting, and in the air fryer it became tender and caramelized. To dress it up, we turned to another winning combination: a glaze of maple syrup and butter, which complemented the drier, savory flesh of the squash. We brushed the mixture, spiced with black pepper and cayenne, on squash wedges before roasting them in the air fryer flesh side up to capture the glaze. Because they overlapped slightly, we rotated the wedges halfway through cooking to ensure evenly browned flesh, then brushed on additional glaze before serving. The wedges were done in just over half an hour, ready to complement a variety of main courses.

2 tablespoons maple syrup

2 tablespoons unsalted butter

Salt and pepper

Pinch cayenne pepper

1 acorn squash (1½ pounds), halved pole to pole and seeded

2 teaspoons fresh thyme leaves

1 Microwave maple syrup, butter, ½ teaspoon salt, ¼ teaspoon pepper, and cayenne in bowl at 50 percent power until butter is melted, about 1 minute, stirring occasionally.

2 Cut each squash half into 4 wedges. Brush flesh of squash wedges with half of syrup mixture. Arrange squash flesh side up in air-fryer basket (squash may overlap slightly). Place basket in air fryer and set temperature to 400 degrees. Cook squash until deep golden brown and tender, 19 to 24 minutes, rotating wedges halfway through cooking.

3 Transfer squash to serving platter, drizzle with remaining syrup mixture, and sprinkle with thyme. Season with salt and pepper to taste. Serve.

BUTTERNUT SQUASH WITH HAZELNUTS AND SAGE

Serves 4

COOK TIME 30 minutes   **TOTAL TIME** 45 minutes

why this recipe works One aspect of the air fryer that we especially came to love is that we could enlist it to cook a side dish while leaving the oven free for the main course. Butternut squash promised a simple but presentation-worthy side. Roasting it in the air fryer brought out its sweetness and tenderness, and a couple of well-chosen ingredients gussied it up. Cutting the squash into 1-inch pieces allowed us to fit a full 6 cups in the basket. The relatively small pieces cooked quickly and were easy to toss, and offered lots of surface area for caramelization, which we boosted by using butter (just 2 tablespoons) instead of oil. For a classic flavor pairing, we added minced fresh sage. Chopped raw hazelnuts brought nutty depth and crunch to our squash; we added them halfway through cooking, allowing them to toast as the squash finished. We prefer to use raw hazelnuts, as toasted hazelnuts can become bitter during cooking. For the best texture it's important to remove the fibrous flesh just below the butternut squash's skin. This dish can be served warm or at room temperature.

2 tablespoons unsalted butter

1 tablespoon minced fresh sage

1 teaspoon lemon juice

Salt and pepper

2 pounds butternut squash, peeled, seeded, and cut into 1-inch pieces (6 cups)

⅓ cup skinned raw hazelnuts, chopped coarse

1 Microwave butter and sage in large bowl at 50 percent power, stirring occasionally, until butter is melted, about 1 minute. Transfer 1 tablespoon butter mixture to small bowl, then stir in lemon juice and ⅛ teaspoon salt; set aside. Add squash, ¼ teaspoon salt, and ⅛ teaspoon pepper to remaining butter mixture and toss to coat.

2 Place squash in air-fryer basket. Place basket in air fryer, set temperature to 400 degrees, and cook for 15 minutes. Stir in hazelnuts and cook until squash is tender and well browned, 15 to 20 minutes, tossing halfway through cooking.

3 Transfer squash mixture to clean large bowl; toss with reserved butter mixture. Season with salt and pepper to taste. Serve.

BUTTERNUT SQUASH WITH ALMONDS AND POMEGRANATE
Omit sage. Substitute chopped raw almonds for hazelnuts. Add ½ cup pomegranate seeds to bowl with reserved butter mixture in step 3.

BUTTERNUT SQUASH WITH PECANS AND ROSEMARY
Substitute chopped raw pecans for hazelnuts and 1½ teaspoons minced fresh rosemary for sage.

ZUCCHINI FRIES

Serves 2 to 4

COOK TIME 10 minutes   **TOTAL TIME** 45 minutes

why this recipe works As summer's bounty of zucchini rolls in, being able to whip up a quick batch of these crispy, salty zucchini fries—a refreshing alternative to their starchier cousins—may be reason enough to keep your air fryer within arm's reach. A combination of toasted panko bread crumbs and grated Parmesan gave us a delightfully crackly and delicate exterior. To adhere the panko mixture to the zucchini, we used a combination of flour and egg seasoned with oregano, salt, and pepper. Zucchini is notoriously watery, so preventing moisture from sogging out the crust was key. Our solution: We cut the zucchini into spears and used a vegetable peeler to quickly remove the watery inner seed pulp. Arranging the fries in a "Lincoln log" pattern in the basket allowed for maximum air circulation. We love these zucchini fries with a simple, bright sauce of yogurt and lemon, but feel free to substitute your favorite marinara sauce. This recipe works best with a single medium zucchini, but larger or smaller zucchini can be used; simply cut the zucchini into ½ by 4-inch sticks (after removing the seeds).

1 zucchini (8 ounces), quartered lengthwise	1 ounce Parmesan cheese, grated (½ cup)	½ teaspoon dried oregano
¾ cup panko bread crumbs	1 large egg	Salt and pepper
2 tablespoons extra-virgin olive oil	1 tablespoon all-purpose flour	½ cup plain yogurt
		½ teaspoon grated lemon zest plus 1 tablespoon juice

1 Using vegetable peeler, shave seeds from inner portion of each zucchini quarter. Halve each quarter lengthwise, then cut in half crosswise. (You should have 16 pieces.)

2 Toss panko with oil in bowl until evenly coated. Microwave, stirring frequently, until light golden brown, 1 to 3 minutes. Transfer to shallow dish, let cool slightly, then stir in Parmesan. Whisk egg, flour, oregano, ¼ teaspoon salt, and ⅛ teaspoon pepper together in second shallow dish. Working with several pieces of zucchini at a time, dredge in egg mixture, letting excess drip off, then coat with panko mixture, pressing gently to adhere; transfer to large plate.

3 Lightly spray base of air-fryer basket with vegetable oil spray. Arrange half of zucchini pieces in prepared basket, spaced evenly apart. Arrange remaining zucchini pieces on top, perpendicular to first layer. Place basket in air fryer and set temperature to 400 degrees. Cook until zucchini is tender and crisp, 10 to 12 minutes, gently shaking basket to loosen pieces halfway through cooking.

4 Meanwhile, whisk yogurt, lemon zest and juice, ¼ teaspoon salt, and ⅛ teaspoon pepper together in small bowl. Transfer zucchini to serving platter and season with salt and pepper to taste. Serve with yogurt sauce.

NUTRITIONAL INFORMATION

To calculate the nutritional values of our recipes per serving, we used The Food Processor SQL by ESHA Research. When using this program, we entered all the ingredients, using weights for important ingredients such as most vegetables. We also used our preferred brands in these analyses. When the recipe called for seasoning with an unspecified amount of salt and pepper, we added ½ teaspoon of salt and ¼ teaspoon of pepper to the analysis. We did not include additional salt or pepper for food that's "seasoned to taste." If there is a range in the serving size, we used the highest number of servings to calculate the nutritional values.

	CALORIES	TOTAL FAT (G)	SAT FAT (G)	CHOL (MG)	CARB (G)	TOTAL SUGAR (G)	ADDED SUGAR (G)	PROTEIN (G)	FIBER (G)	SODIUM (G)
Chicken										
Chicken Parmesan	700	32	9	285	30	4	0	67	2	1100
Chicken Nuggets	690	24	4.5	305	51	2	0	63	2	910
Sweet-and-Sour Dipping Sauce	150	0	0	0	39	36	0	0	0	40
Honey-Dijon Dipping Sauce	90	0	0	0	17	16	16	0	0	720
Nut-Crusted Chicken Breasts	660	34	10	290	24	2	0	62	4	1040
Spicy Fried-Chicken Sandwich	520	23	4	135	42	5	0	34	2	1210
Apricot-Thyme Glazed Chicken Breasts	340	8	1.5	165	13	9	0	51	0	400
Pineapple-Ginger Glazed Chicken Breasts	340	8	1.5	165	13	12	0	51	0	390
Unstuffed Chicken Breasts with Dijon Mayonnaise	550	27	9	220	1	1	0	70	0	1500
Spiced Chicken Breasts with Asparagus, Arugula, and Cannellini Bean Salad	550	20	3.5	165	29	6	0	63	10	1180
Roasted Bone-In Chicken Breasts	490	28	8	175	0	0	0	57	0	460
Peach-Ginger Chutney	140	2.5	0	0	30	27	13	1	2	150
Lemon-Basil Salsa Verde	200	21	3	0	2	0	0	1	1	320
Roasted Bone-In Chicken Breasts and Fingerling Potatoes with Sun-Dried Tomato Relish	730	32	8	175	46	2	0	62	7	1050
Barbecued Bone-In Chicken Breasts with Creamy Coleslaw	660	40	10	185	14	7	1	58	2	790
Pomegranate-Glazed Bone-In Chicken Breasts with Couscous Salad	910	43	11	185	62	27	2	66	3	980
Air-Fried Chicken	670	28	8	175	39	5	0	62	2	1330
Thai Cornish Game Hens with Cucumber Salad	900	59	15	350	24	16	13	65	3	670
Teriyaki Chicken with Snow Peas	620	40	11	235	19	12	6	43	2	610
Tandoori Chicken Thighs	610	45	12	245	7	3	0	43	1	560
Shredded Chicken Tacos	440	16	6	130	44	6	0	33	7	590
Thai-Style Chicken Lettuce Wraps	290	11	2	105	22	15	2	27	4	290

	CALORIES	TOTAL FAT (G)	SAT FAT (G)	CHOL (MG)	CARB (G)	TOTAL SUGAR (G)	ADDED SUGAR (G)	PROTEIN (G)	FIBER (G)	SODIUM (G)
Chicken (cont.)										
Jerk Chicken Leg Quarters	500	31	8	230	11	7	7	43	1	800
Paprika-Rubbed Chicken Drumsticks	350	20	5	175	5	2	2	35	1	790
Buffalo Chicken Drumsticks	480	33	13	210	7	5	5	36	1	1420
Turkey Burgers	340	8	5	60	29	6	0	38	2	700
Turkey Burgers with Sun-Dried Tomatoes and Basil	370	10	6	60	32	6	0	38	2	740
Mini Glazed Turkey Meatloaves	580	29	6	260	31	18	7	48	1	980
Beef, Pork, and Lamb										
Spice-Rubbed Steak with Snap Pea and Cucumber Salad	530	39	12	135	8	3	0	36	3	990
Top Sirloin Steak with Roasted Mushrooms and Blue Cheese Sauce	450	25	10	135	10	6	0	43	1	860
Flank Steak with Roasted Potatoes and Chimichurri	660	36	9	115	43	8	5	41	4	720
Korean Steak Tips with Napa Cabbage Slaw	470	26	7	115	19	13	8	39	3	600
Coffee- and Fennel-Rubbed Boneless Short Ribs with Celery Root Salad	650	34	10	100	49	15	2	40	10	950
Roasted Boneless Short Ribs with Red Pepper Relish	400	27	9	100	5	3	2	33	1	510
Ginger-Soy Beef and Vegetable Kebabs	560	38	8	115	15	10	4	40	2	1310
Beef Satay with Red Curry Noodles	680	27	15	105	64	11	7	44	5	840
Big Italian Meatballs with Zucchini Noodles	650	31	11	250	28	13	0	63	5	1540
Juicy Well-Done Cheeseburgers	580	32	13	130	28	5	0	41	1	900
Juicy Well-Done Green Chile Cheeseburgers	640	37	15	140	29	5	0	44	2	940
Juicy Well-Done Burgers with Caramelized Onions and Blue Cheese	620	35	14	130	31	6	0	41	2	850
Steak Tacos	530	24	7	85	48	7	1	32	10	520
Southwestern Beef Hand Pies	480	29	13	115	34	0	0	23	1	760
Southwestern Bean and Corn Hand Pies	510	29	12	80	52	3	0	15	5	1020
Crispy Breaded Boneless Pork Chops	570	22	11	275	26	1	0	58	1	850
Roasted Bone-In Pork Chop	210	9	2.5	75	0	0	0	30	0	370
Peach-Mustard Sauce	50	0	0	0	13	12	6	1	1	40
Chermoula	340	37	5	0	2	0	0	0	1	0
Lemon-Oregano Roasted Pork Chops with Tomato-Feta Salad	620	34	10	175	20	14	5	58	3	970
Fennel-Rubbed Pork Tenderloin with Zucchini Ribbon Salad	500	27	14	230	0	0	0	60	0	900
Pork Tenderloin with Prosciutto and Sage	500	24	6	160	13	8	4	56	3	830
Sweet and Smoky Pork Tenderloin with Butternut Squash	490	15	6	160	39	14	9	53	6	860

	CALORIES	TOTAL FAT (G)	SAT FAT (G)	CHOL (MG)	CARB (G)	TOTAL SUGAR (G)	ADDED SUGAR (G)	PROTEIN (G)	FIBER (G)	SODIUM (G)
Beef, Pork, and Lamb (cont.)										
Vietnamese-Style Rice Noodle Salad with Pork	400	7	1	75	55	5	3	30	2	500
Polynesian Pork Kebabs with Pineapple and Onion	510	24	5	125	35	25	4	39	4	1040
Italian Sausage and Pepper Subs	440	18	5	35	45	12	3	25	7	1160
Mustard-Thyme Lamb Chops with Roasted Carrots	430	19	4.5	100	29	18	8	34	6	860
Lamb Sliders with Apricot Chutney	670	36	16	110	58	21	4	36	4	760
Lamb Sliders with Smoky Tomato Relish	630	37	16	115	45	7	0	35	3	850
Lamb Kofte Wraps	550	37	19	115	24	5	0	33	2	720
Lamb Meatballs with Couscous	670	35	16	115	54	16	0	35	5	760
Seafood										
Better-Than-Boxed Fish Sticks	430	17	2.5	195	29	1	0	35	1	990
Tartar Sauce	70	7	2	5	1	1	0	1	0	210
Old Bay Dipping Sauce	70	7	2	5	1	1	0	1	0	110
Crunchy Air-Fried Cod Fillets	340	12	2	190	12	1	0	43	1	490
Creamy Chipotle Chile Sauce	230	25	5	25	2	1	0	1	0	190
Roasted Cod with Lemon-Garlic Potatoes	490	19	11	145	33	1	0	44	3	710
Moroccan Spiced Halibut with Chickpea Salad	470	17	2.5	110	30	5	1	50	9	910
Sole and Asparagus Bundles with Tarragon Butter	380	29	15	135	6	3	0	24	2	500
Roasted Salmon Fillets	500	34	7	125	0	0	0	46	0	430
Herb-Yogurt Sauce	40	2	1.5	10	4	3	0	2	0	30
Mango-Mint Salsa	150	8	1	0	20	3	0	0	1	360
Orange-Mustard Glazed Salmon	520	32	7	125	8	7	0	46	0	550
Honey-Chipotle Glazed Salmon	550	32	7	125	18	16	16	47	0	430
Hoisin Glazed Salmon	520	32	7	125	8	4	0	47	1	680
Salmon Tacos with Roasted Pineapple Slaw	600	29	4.5	60	59	13	0	30	12	330
Swordfish Skewers with Tomato-Scallion Caponata	460	26	5	110	21	13	5	37	7	940
Crab Cakes with Bibb Lettuce and Apple Salad	350	16	2.5	225	17	8	0	32	3	780
Thai Shrimp Skewers with Peanut Dipping Sauce	340	21	3	215	10	5	3	29	2	770
Bacon-Wrapped Scallops with Spinach, Fennel, and Raspberry Salad	540	42	12	75	16	6	1	24	6	950
South Carolina-Style Shrimp Bake	410	18	5	200	31	4	0	34	3	880

	CALORIES	TOTAL FAT (G)	SAT FAT (G)	CHOL (MG)	CARB (G)	TOTAL SUGAR (G)	ADDED SUGAR (G)	PROTEIN (G)	FIBER (G)	SODIUM (G)
Vegetables										
Roasted Asparagus	30	1.5	0	0	3	2	0	2	2	75
Mint-Orange Gremolata	30	1.5	0	0	4	2	0	2	2	75
Tarragon-Lemon Gremolata	30	1.5	0	0	4	2	0	2	2	75
Air-Fried Brussels Sprouts	80	4	0.5	0	9	2	0	3	4	170
Air-Fried Brussels Sprouts with Crispy Shallots	90	4	0.5	0	13	4	0	4	5	170
Lemon-Chive Dipping Sauce	90	10	1.5	5	1	0	0	0	0	115
Orange-Cardamom Roasted Carrots	150	6	3.5	15	24	14	4	2	6	280
Cumin-Lime Roasted Carrots	150	6	3.5	15	24	14	4	2	6	290
Smoked Paprika–Lemon Roasted Carrots	150	6	3.5	15	24	14	4	2	6	290
Curried Roasted Cauliflower and Chickpea Salad	290	19	2.5	0	29	9	0	10	9	420
Roasted Green Beans with Sun-Dried Tomatoes and Sunflower Seeds	160	11	3	5	11	4	0	7	4	170
Roasted Bell Pepper Salad with Mozzarella and Basil	300	23	6	20	13	9	0	7	3	230
Roasted Bell Pepper Salad with Manchego and Olives	300	26	6	10	12	6	0	7	4	510
Baked Potatoes	180	1	0	0	41	1	0	5	3	160
Blue Cheese–Pepper Butter	90	9	6	25	0	0	0	1	0	50
Lemon-Thyme Butter	100	11	7	30	0	0	0	0	0	0
Crispy Smashed Potatoes	180	7	1	0	27	2	0	3	3	320
Crispy Smashed Potatoes with Garlic and Dill	180	7	1	0	27	2	0	3	3	320
Cheesy Potatoes	380	18	11	50	43	1	0	15	3	610
French Fries	200	7	0.5	0	31	1	0	4	2	300
Sriracha Dipping Sauce	100	10	1.5	5	1	1	0	0	0	170
Parmesan, Rosemary, and Black Pepper French Fries	240	10	2	10	31	1	0	8	2	340
BBQ Potato Wedges	200	7	0.5	0	32	2	1	4	3	320
Latin Potato Wedges	200	7	0.5	0	31	1	0	4	3	320
Steakhouse Potato Wedges	200	7	0.5	0	31	1	0	4	3	300
Maple-Glazed Acorn Squash	130	6	3.5	15	20	9	6	1	2	300
Butternut Squash with Hazelnuts and Sage	210	13	4	15	24	5	0	4	5	230
Butternut Squash with Almonds and Pomegranates	230	12	4	15	29	8	0	5	6	230
Butternut Squash with Pecans and Rosemary	190	12	4	15	24	5	0	3	5	230
Zucchini Fries	210	12	3	55	16	3	0	8	1	480

CONVERSIONS AND EQUIVALENTS

Some say cooking is a science and an art. We would say that geography has a hand in it, too. Flours and sugars manufactured in the United Kingdom and elsewhere will feel and taste different from those manufactured in the United States. So we cannot promise that the loaf of bread you bake in Canada or England will taste the same as a loaf baked in the States, but we can offer guidelines for converting weights and measures. We also recommend that you rely on your instincts when making our recipes. Refer to the visual cues provided. If the dough hasn't "come together in a ball" as described, you may need to add more flour—even if the recipe doesn't tell you to. You be the judge.

The recipes in this book were developed using standard U.S. measures following U.S. government guidelines. The charts below offer equivalents for U.S. and metric measures. All conversions are approximate and have been rounded up or down to the nearest whole number.

Example

1 teaspoon	=	4.9292 milliliters, rounded up to 5 milliliters
1 ounce	=	28.3495 grams, rounded down to 28 grams

Volume Conversions

U.S.	METRIC
1 teaspoon	5 milliliters
2 teaspoons	10 milliliters
1 tablespoon	15 milliliters
2 tablespoons	30 milliliters
¼ cup	59 milliliters
⅓ cup	79 milliliters
½ cup	118 milliliters
¾ cup	177 milliliters
1 cup	237 milliliters
1¼ cups	296 milliliters
1½ cups	355 milliliters
2 cups (1 pint)	473 milliliters
2½ cups	591 milliliters
3 cups	710 milliliters
4 cups (1 quart)	0.946 liter
1.06 quarts	1 liter
4 quarts (1 gallon)	3.8 liters

Weight Conversions

OUNCES	GRAMS
½	14
¾	21
1	28
1½	43
2	57
2½	71
3	85
3½	99
4	113
4½	128
5	142
6	170
7	198
8	227
9	255
10	283
12	340
16 (1 pound)	454

Conversions for Common Baking Ingredients

Baking is an exacting science. Because measuring by weight is far more accurate than measuring by volume, and thus more likely to produce reliable results, in our recipes we provide ounce measures in addition to cup measures for many ingredients. Refer to the chart below to convert these measures into grams.

INGREDIENT	OUNCES	GRAMS
flour		
1 cup all-purpose flour*	5	142
1 cup cake flour	4	113
1 cup whole-wheat flour	5½	156
sugar		
1 cup granulated (white) sugar	7	198
1 cup packed brown sugar (light or dark)	7	198
1 cup confectioners' sugar	4	113
cocoa powder		
1 cup cocoa powder	3	85
butter†		
4 tablespoons (½ stick or ¼ cup)	2	57
8 tablespoons (1 stick or ½ cup)	4	113
16 tablespoons (2 sticks or 1 cup)	8	227

* U.S. all-purpose flour, the most frequently used flour in this book, does not contain leaveners, as some European flours do. These leavened flours are called self-rising or self-raising. If you are using self-rising flour, take this into consideration before adding leaveners to a recipe.

† In the United States, butter is sold both salted and unsalted. We generally recommend unsalted butter. If you are using salted butter, take this into consideration before adding salt to a recipe.

Oven Temperatures

FAHRENHEIT	CELSIUS	GAS MARK
225	105	¼
250	120	½
275	135	1
300	150	2
325	165	3
350	180	4
375	190	5
400	200	6
425	220	7
450	230	8
475	245	9

Converting Temperatures from an Instant-Read Thermometer

We include doneness temperatures in many of the recipes in this book. We recommend an instant-read thermometer for the job. Refer to the table above to convert Fahrenheit degrees to Celsius. Or, for temperatures not represented in the chart, use this simple formula:

Subtract 32 degrees from the Fahrenheit reading, then divide the result by 1.8 to find the Celsius reading.

Example:
"Roast chicken until thighs register 175 degrees."
To convert:
$$175°F - 32 = 143°$$
$$143° ÷ 1.8 = 79.44°C, \text{ rounded down to } 79°C$$

INDEX

Note: Page references in *italics* indicate photographs.